AQA

GCSE Health & Social Care

Adrian Lamb

Philip Allan Updates, part of the Hodder Education Group, an Hachette Livre UK company, Market Place, Deddington, Oxfordshire OX15 0SE

Orders
Bookpoint Ltd, 130 Milton Park, Abingdon, Oxfordshire, OX14 4SB
tel: 01235 827720   fax: 01235 400454
e-mail: uk.orders@bookpoint.co.uk
Lines are open 9.00 a.m.–5.00 p.m., Monday to Saturday, with a 24-hour message answering service. You can also order through the Philip Allan Updates website: www.philipallan.co.uk

© Philip Allan Updates 2007

ISBN 978-1-84489-619-6

All rights reserved; no part of this publication may be reproduced, stored in a retrieval system, or transmitted, in any form or by any means, electronic, mechanical, photocopying, recording or otherwise without either the prior written permission of Philip Allan Updates or a licence permitting restricted copying in the United Kingdom issued by the Copyright Licensing Agency Ltd, Saffron House, 6–10 Kirby Street, London EC1N 8TS.

Printed in Malaysia

Philip Allan Updates' policy is to use papers that are natural, renewable and recyclable products and made from wood grown in sustainable forests. The logging and manufacturing processes are expected to conform to the environmental regulations of the country of origin.

Contents

Introduction
About this book iv
Assessment objectives v

Unit 1 Health, social care & early years provision
Care needs of major client groups 3
Types of care service 7
Obtaining care services and barriers to access 15
Job roles in health, social care and early years services 18
The value bases of care work 37
The assessment requirements 46

Unit 2 Promoting health and well-being
What is health and well-being? 51
Positive factors affecting health and well-being 52
Factors causing risks to health and well-being 67
Indicators of physical health 86
Motivating and supporting individuals to improve their health 92
The assessment requirements 93

Unit 3 Understanding personal development and relationships
Human growth and development 97
Factors that affect growth and development 112
Relationships and personal development 122
Factors that influence self-concept 124
The effects of life events on personal development 125
The assessment requirements 130

Index 131

Introduction

About this book

This book has been written to help you enjoy and succeed on the AQA GCSE Health and Social Care course. It is an Applied GCSE course in which the successful candidates achieve a double GCSE award. The course is divided into three different units and the marks gained on each one are added together to give a final total, which will determine the grade achieved. The book is organised into three sections to match the three units of the specification. These are:

1 Health, social care & early years provision
2 Promoting health and well-being
3 Understanding personal development and relationships

Units 1 and 2 require you to produce and submit material in the form of a portfolio. Your portfolio evidence must be your own work and should be organised carefully to meet the assessment requirements. Unit 3 is assessed through a written test of 90 minutes. The test is made up of different types of question. Some need short answers, while others require longer pieces of writing, and will need to be planned carefully before answering.

Read through the book, try the activities and follow the advice on assessment. This will help you to:
+ prepare for progression to employment or further education and training
+ increase your knowledge and understanding of the health, social care and early years topics
+ develop an awareness of the influences affecting an individual's health and well-being
+ recognise the importance of the stages of development for the individual and his/her relationships
+ develop a critical and analytical approach to problem-solving in health and social care contexts

Assessment objectives

There are three different assessment objectives. In Units 1 and 2 you will be assessed on all three. You should be able to:
+ recall and apply knowledge, skills and understanding
+ plan and carry out investigations and tasks
+ evaluate evidence, make reasoned judgements and present conclusions

In Unit 3, only the first and last of the three objectives will be tested — there will be no questions that test planning and carrying out investigations and tasks.

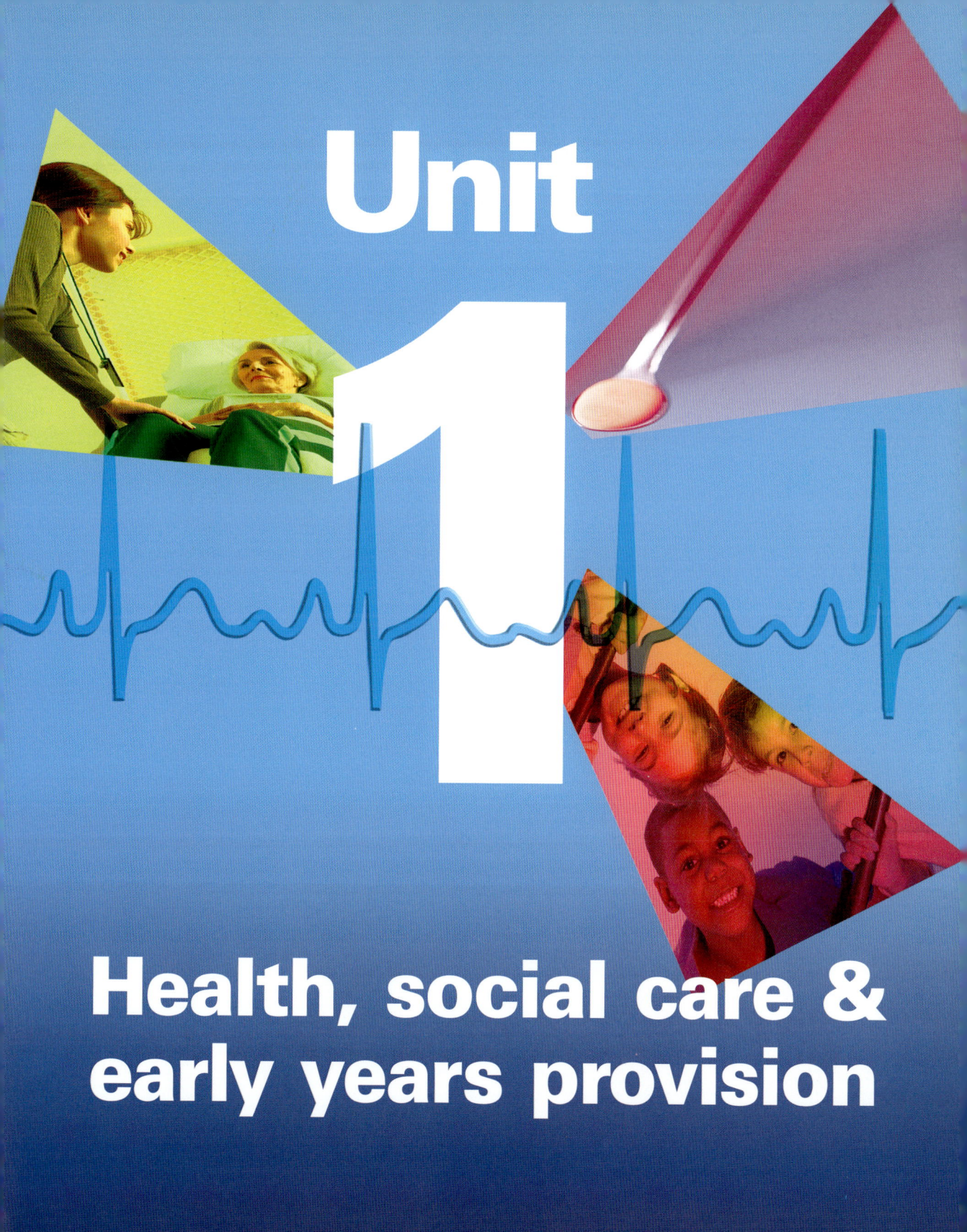

Unit 1
Health, social care & early years provision

This unit covers:
+ the range of care needs of major client groups
+ the types of service that exist to meet client group needs and how they are organised
+ the ways people can obtain care services and the barriers that can prevent people from gaining access to services
+ the main work roles and skills of people who provide health, social care and early years services
+ the values that underpin all care work and clients

You need to learn:
+ who needs to use care services and why
+ what types of care service are provided to meet the needs of client groups
+ how people can gain access to care services and what can prevent people from being able to use the services that they need
+ what care work involves and the skills that care practitioners need in order to perform their work roles
+ the values that care workers promote through their work

Care needs of major client groups

From when we are born up to 10 years of age we develop from babies into children. At 11 we become adolescents and at 19 years of age we are adults. We stay in this adult life stage until the age of 65, after which we might be classed as older people. Older people can also be called

Unit 1

Health, social care & early years provision

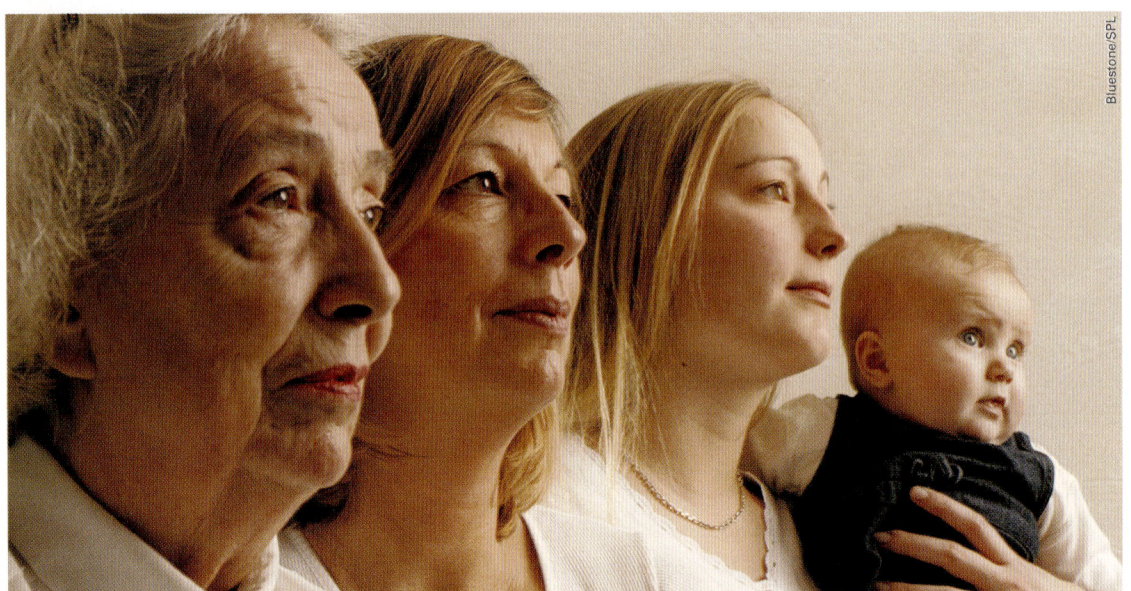

Our care needs change as we get older

elderly people, or people in later adulthood. At any age, some individuals may be disabled. The care needs of individuals in these different client groups change as they grow older, and may be different if they are disabled.

Our health needs can be thought of as physical, intellectual, emotional and social (PIES).

Physical needs

Physical needs are the needs of our bodies. Physically, we need an appropriate diet, warmth, shelter and safety to avoid illness and accidents. Having enough to eat is important as we need food materials for growth and energy. If we have too little food, we feel tired and cold. If we eat too much, we put on weight and may suffer from some weight-related illness.

We need to be warm so that our bodies can function properly. If we get cold by being exposed to low temperatures, our bodies may not be able to replace the heat that we lose to the surroundings. Under these conditions, our body temperature drops below the normal 35°. Shivering occurs and 'goose bumps' form on the skin. These are normal reactions to being cold. We can become pale and our lips, ears, fingers and toes may turn blue. If it is very cold, the normal processes of the cells shut down, which can cause major organ failure. This can lead to death from **hypothermia**.

Having appropriate shelter gives us protection from the weather in a place where we are comfortable and safe.

Intellectual needs

Intellectual needs are the needs of our minds. These are sometimes called mental needs. Intellectually, we need stimulation to learn and avoid boredom. Learning is a process that continues throughout our lives. It begins before we go to school — we gain knowledge and understanding from parents and other family members. Education helps us to modify our attitudes and behaviour. We gain skills and values through study and life experiences. Starting work provides intellectual stimulation as we learn what our jobs require of us. In our spare time, activities such as reading newspapers and magazines, doing quizzes or simply watching television programmes all add to our understanding.

Emotional needs

Emotional needs are to do with our feelings. Emotionally, we need to develop our **self-concept** (how we see ourselves), and we develop through experiencing a range of feelings.

As individuals, we are all different. We share the same basic needs but the strength of a need may vary in different people. In much the same way that some people need more food or more sleep (physical needs), some have greater emotional needs. When emotional needs are not met, individuals may feel frustrated. Over a period of time, continuing frustration when needs are not met can lead to mental health problems. It is natural for people to need to feel:

- accepted
- appreciated
- challenged
- forgiven and forgiving
- helped and helpful
- included
- loved
- productive/useful
- respected
- treated fairly
- valued
- acknowledged
- approved of
- competent
- free
- important
- listened to
- needed
- reassured
- safe/secure
- understood
- worthy
- admired
- capable
- confident
- fulfilled
- in control
- not confused
- noticed
- recognised
- supported
- understanding

> **Definitions**
> **Self-concept**, **self-awareness** or **self-identify** is how we see ourselves.

Social needs

Social needs involve interactions with other people. Socially, we need to interact with other individuals in society to avoid isolation.

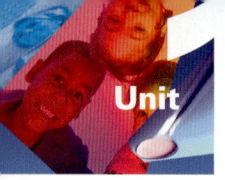

Unit 1

Health, social care & early years provision

We develop socially by interacting with family, friends and people we meet at work and in leisure time. Social skills develop as we learn how to interact with others in appropriate ways. Some of the important social skills are:

- having the ability to stay relaxed in social situations
- being a good listener
- showing interest in others
- showing **empathy** for others
- building a **rapport** with others
- knowing when to speak and how much to say
- using appropriate **body language**

Social and emotional needs are often closely linked. Our interactions with others affect the way we feel. For example, if we are alone for long periods, we become isolated and feel lonely.

Good health and well-being require that all of these PIES needs are met. People are developing continuously, no matter how old they are. Physical growth may stop, but individuals need to maintain and repair their bodies. Intellectually, we are never too old to learn, while emotionally and socially our needs change as we enter or leave work, become parents or grandparents and choose different lifestyles.

It is important to remember that while we are all individuals with many needs in common, our needs vary from person to person. Even identical twins may have different needs, depending on lifestyle choices and personal circumstances.

> **Definitions**
>
> **Body language** is communicating using body movements or gestures, e.g. eye contact.
>
> **Empathy** is being able to put yourself in the other person's shoes — to feel his/her emotion.
>
> **Rapport** is being on the same wavelength as the person you are talking to.

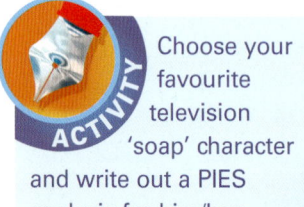

ACTIVITY Choose your favourite television 'soap' character and write out a PIES analysis for him/her.

Our needs vary from person to person and can depend, among other things, on lifestyle choices

6

AQA GCSE **Health & Social Care**

Providing and developing services

Health and social care services are provided by health authorities and local authorities. Services are provided and developed to meet **health and social policy goals**, which aim to improve human welfare, including health services and living conditions.

Examples of these include services to reduce child **poverty**, help the homeless and reduce drug misuse in the population.

It is important that the authorities are able to find out how great the needs are in their local area and are able to provide services and develop these should these needs change.

Social care issues

Child poverty Children living in poverty are more likely to play truant from school and get into trouble with the law. Later in life they are more likely to be unemployed and earn lower wages when they are in work. 'Sure start' is an example of a government initiative to tackle child poverty.

Homelessness can be caused by unemployment, when individuals cannot afford to pay for their home when they lose their job. Sometimes it can be the other way round — becoming homeless can lead to a person becoming unemployed. The effects of homelessness often include poor access to medical services, feelings of insecurity and individuals feeling harassed and discriminated against. This can lead to loss of self-esteem, increased danger of abuse and violence, and development of behavioural problems.

Shelter is an organisation that aims to tackle the problems of homelessness.

Drug abuse Individuals who misuse drugs are likely to become addicted. This means that they crave the drug and become dependent on it. If they do not receive the drug, addicts can suffer physical and emotional symptoms of withdrawal. Common problems linked to drug abuse include increased levels of anxiety, depression, disrupted rest and sleep, and irritability. The National Drugs Helpline offers free help and advice, 24 hours a day, 7 days a week, for both drug abusers and their relatives and friends.

FIND IT OUT What does Shelter do in your area?

Types of care service

Services are provided for healthcare, social care and for early years. These services are either statutory or non-statutory. **Statutory care services** are those that the law says must be provided. **Non-statutory services** do not have to be provided by law. The different services are found in four different sectors. There are two statutory service sectors — the National Health Service (NHS) and local authorities — and two non-statutory service sectors — private and voluntary.

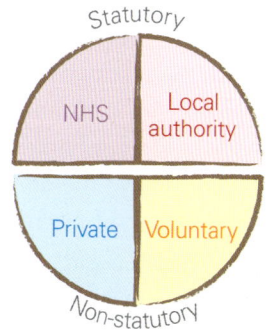

The four service sectors

7

Unit 1

Health, social care & early years provision

Non-statutory services can be provided by private organisations or individuals working to make a profit, or by voluntary organisations or individuals who work without pay to provide free services.

The National Health Service (NHS)

The National Health Service is a statutory service that provides a variety of health services across the country.

The National Health Service (NHS)

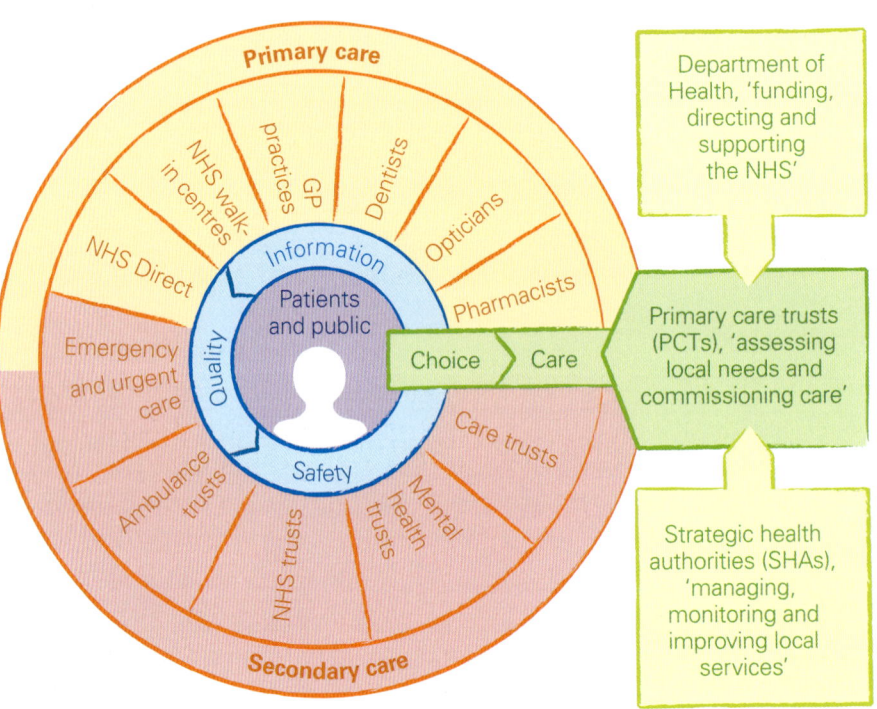

The Department of Health is the part of the government that sets and monitors health and social care provision. The Secretary of State for Health works with five Ministers for Health. The Secretary of State is accountable to Parliament for the work of the NHS. The Department of Health focuses on providing strategic leadership for the NHS and social care organisation. This includes:

+ setting overall direction
+ ensuring national standards are met
+ securing resources
+ making major investment decisions
+ improving choice for patients and users

8

AQA GCSE **Health & Social Care**

Strategic health authorities

There are 28 strategic health authorities in England, which develop strategies for local health services and monitor their work. This means that the strategic health authorities manage the NHS locally. Each authority covers a population of around 1.5 million. They are the key link between the Department of Health and the NHS. Each strategic health authority makes sure that:

+ national priorities are integrated into the plans of local health services
+ coherent strategies are developed to improve local health services
+ high-quality performance of the local health service is achieved
+ capacity in the local health service will meet future demands

Special health authorities

Special health authorities provide services across all of England — for example, the National Blood Authority and NHS Direct. NHS Direct is an advice line that is available 24 hours a day.

Primary care trusts

Primary care trusts (PCTs) are the first point of contact for most people with health needs. There are around 300 PCTs in England and Wales serving their local communities. Each primary care trust covers a population of approximately 150 000–300 000 people. The PCTs are responsible for planning and securing services appropriate for local needs — for example, making sure there are sufficient general practitioners (GPs) to provide for the local population and that they are accessible to patients.

The PCTs also have a **commissioning** role. This means they determine the volume and quality of services provided by hospitals, walk-in centres, NHS Direct, dentists, mental health services, patient transport, population screening, pharmacies and opticians. Some of these services may be provided directly by the PCT while others may be provided by local service agreements with other organisations, such as hospitals.

As well as improving the health of the local community, PCTs are responsible for ensuring that NHS organisations work together with local authorities. This means that health and social care services can be integrated in the local community.

> **Definition**
> **Commissioning** is the process in the NHS by which different patient services are ordered and paid for.

Other trusts

There are other trusts that work alongside the PCTs. NHS trusts (sometimes called acute trusts) manage hospitals that provide emergency and planned

Unit 1

Health, social care & early years provision

The NHS organisational structure

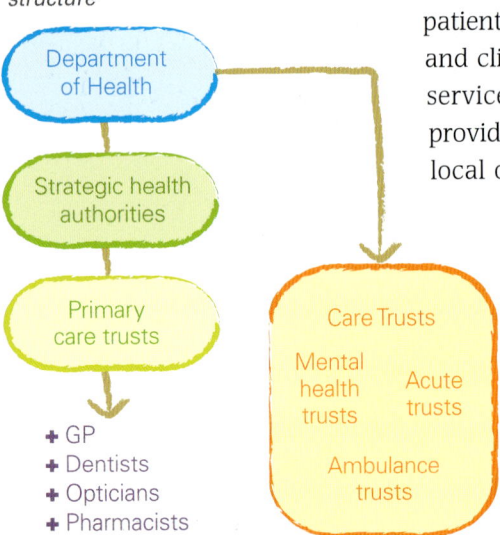

- GP
- Dentists
- Opticians
- Pharmacists
- Walk-in-centres

Definition

Counselling is help from a trained therapist who listens to clients' problems and advises them on how to find their own answers without being judged.

Psychological therapy is the different treatment of mental and emotional disorders involving counselling.

ACTIVITY What NHS services are available in your local community? Draw a simple diagram of your local area to show the location of NHS services and what they offer.

treatment. It is through the NHS trusts that PCTs commission or purchase services such as treatments in the hospital where individuals are in-patients or attend for day surgery, out-patient consultations and clinics. The NHS trusts employ the majority of health service workers. There are 176 acute trusts in England providing medical and surgical care. Ambulance trusts are local organisations that respond to emergency 999 calls; they provide paramedic service and transport for patients to hospital. There are 33 ambulance trusts in England.

Mental health trusts provide specialist care such as **psychological therapy** and **counselling** for individuals with mental health needs. They often work in partnership with local authority social services. There are 88 mental health trusts in England. Specialist care is provided in cases where individuals suffer from depression, stress, anxiety, or the effects of bereavement.

Care trusts combine NHS health and social care services under a single structure to help individuals, such as the elderly, who often have both health and social care needs. There are relatively few care trusts at the present time, but their numbers are expected to increase.

Patient choice is an important aspect of NHS care. Patients have more control than ever before about appointment times and dates and where they get their treatment. This means treatment can fit in with a patient's family and work commitments and can be easily accessible.

Social services

Social services are statutory services organised by local authorities. They often work in partnership with health services to meet the needs of children and adults who are vulnerable. The services provided may be in hospitals, health centres, educational settings, community groups, residential homes, advice centres or in clients' own homes.

Victoria Climbié was a child murder victim. She was only 8 years old and had suffered severe physical abuse and neglect over a period of several months. She was tortured to death by her great-aunt and

AQA GCSE Health & Social Care

the woman's boyfriend. Police, doctors and social workers all had contact with the girl while she was being abused, but they failed to save her. Following her tragic death, the government produced a report called *Every Child Matters – Change for Children*. The government's aim is that every child and young person from birth up to the age of 19 will have the support they need to:

+ be healthy
+ stay safe
+ enjoy and achieve
+ make a positive contribution
+ achieve economic well-being

As a result of this report, children's and young people's services have been reorganised. Here is an example of how social services for children and young people may now be structured.

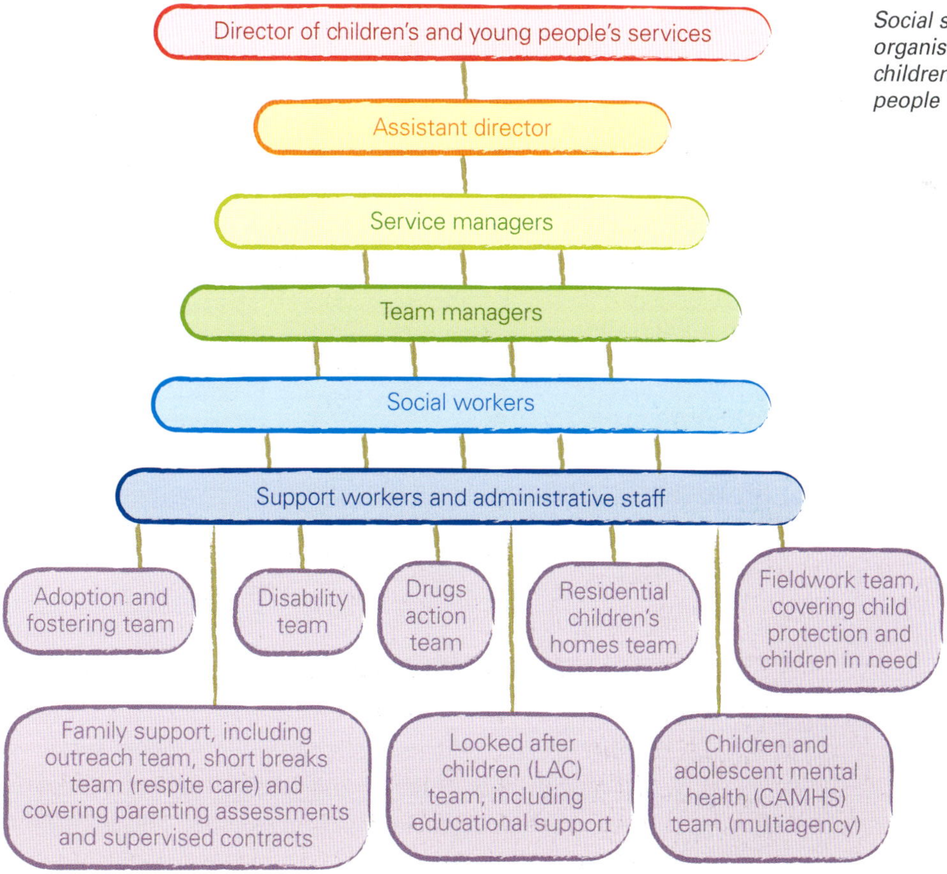

Social services organisation for children and young people

- Director of children's and young people's services
- Assistant director
- Service managers
- Team managers
- Social workers
- Support workers and administrative staff

- Adoption and fostering team
- Disability team
- Drugs action team
- Residential children's homes team
- Fieldwork team, covering child protection and children in need
- Family support, including outreach team, short breaks team (respite care) and covering parenting assessments and supervised contracts
- Looked after children (LAC) team, including educational support
- Children and adolescent mental health (CAMHS) team (multiagency)

Unit 1

Health, social care & early years provision

Adult social services are organised differently. Teams of social workers and support staff work with vulnerable older people and adults who have physical disabilities, learning disabilities and mental health needs. They also support family, friends and other carers who look after these adults. The overall aim is to help individuals live as independently as possible. Here is an example of how adult social services may be organised.

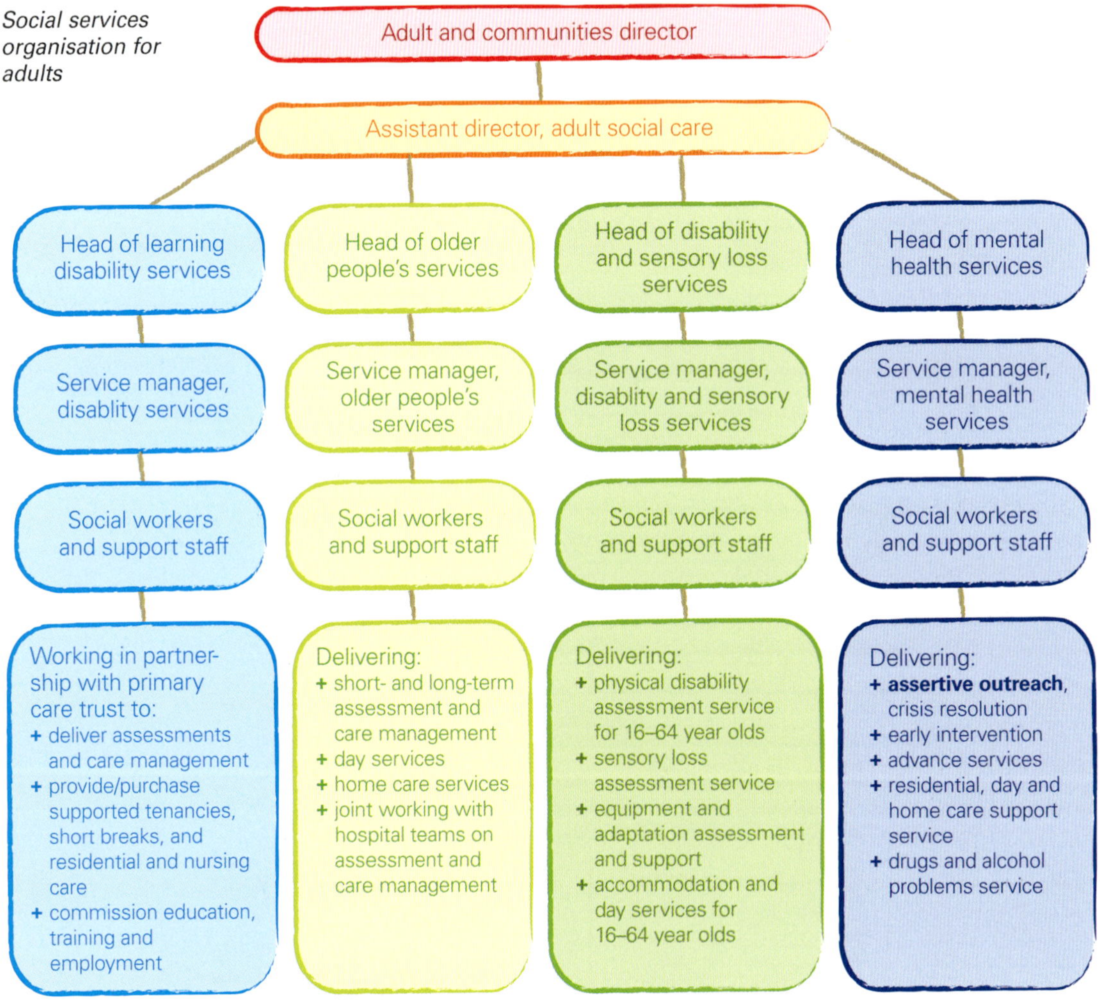

Social services organisation for adults

- **Adult and communities director**
  - **Assistant director, adult social care**
    - **Head of learning disability services**
      - Service manager, disability services
      - Social workers and support staff
      - Working in partnership with primary care trust to:
        + deliver assessments and care management
        + provide/purchase supported tenancies, short breaks, and residential and nursing care
        + commission education, training and employment
    - **Head of older people's services**
      - Service manager, older people's services
      - Social workers and support staff
      - Delivering:
        + short- and long-term assessment and care management
        + day services
        + home care services
        + joint working with hospital teams on assessment and care management
    - **Head of disability and sensory loss services**
      - Service manager, disability and sensory loss services
      - Social workers and support staff
      - Delivering:
        + physical disability assessment service for 16–64 year olds
        + sensory loss assessment service
        + equipment and adaptation assessment and support
        + accommodation and day services for 16–64 year olds
    - **Head of mental health services**
      - Service manager, mental health services
      - Social workers and support staff
      - Delivering:
        + **assertive outreach**, crisis resolution
        + early intervention
        + advance services
        + residential, day and home care support service
        + drugs and alcohol problems service

> **Definition**
> **Assertive outreach** is a way to help people with severe mental health problems in their own homes.

Other social services, such as family support services, work with both children and adults. The focus today is very much on agencies working together. This is called a multi-agency approach.

12

AQA GCSE Health & Social Care

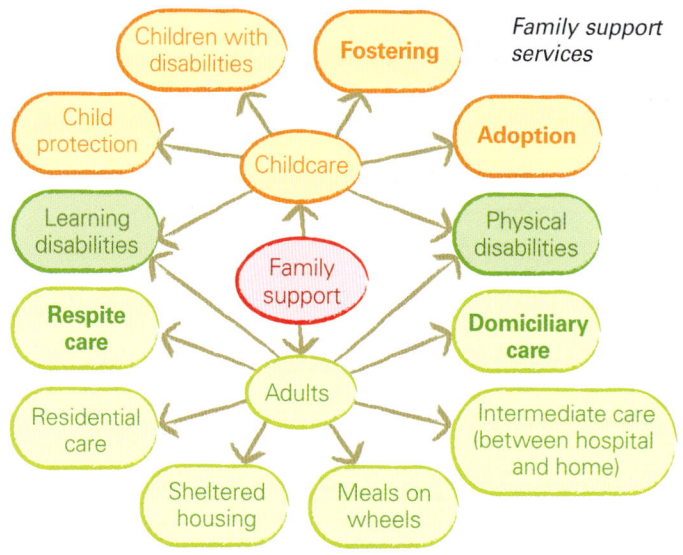

Definitions

Adoption is the legal act of permanently placing a child with a parent or parents other than the birth parents.

Domiciliary care means care at home.

Fostering is acting as a parent or guardian in place of a child's natural parents but without legally adopting the child.

Respite care is temporary residential care for a patient, which provides a break for the main care givers. This is often needed for disabled or terminally ill patients who are cared for at home by their families.

Multi-agency working

Clients' needs are best met when different services work together. For example, for a young child with a difficult family background, who is having problems with education, social services and education staff from both the school and the local authority will work together to help that child.

All authorities that provide care services have to work within the financial limits set by the amount of money they have available. They assess local needs to work out how much of a particular service they should provide. This can be very hard to get right. Some people may have to wait to get the service they need. For example, waiting lists for non-emergency operations are affected by the changing number of emergency operations that have to be performed. Waiting lists for the same service can differ between areas. This is sometimes called the '**postcode lottery**'. However, everybody has equal access to emergency services because their life may depend on it.

Private care services

Private care services are non-statutory services. Private care providers are individuals and companies who provide care services for payment. They aim to make a profit from the services they provide. Clients with non-emergency health needs are able to avoid NHS hospital waiting lists if

13

Unit 1
Health, social care & early years provision

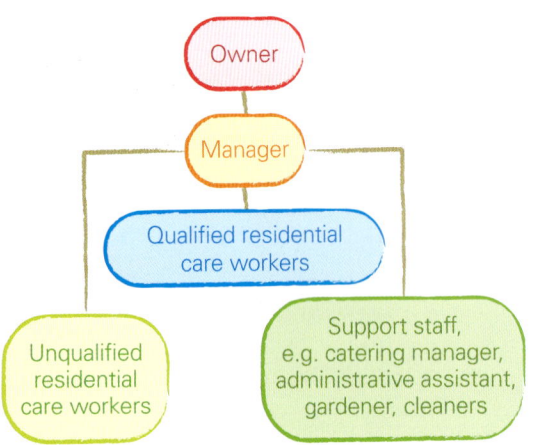

The typical organisation of a private residential home for children

they can pay or they have medical insurance. Large private organisations such as BUPA provide hospital services and care homes, and sell health insurance. Smaller organisations, such as local care homes, may have a much simpler structure.

For people with social care needs, private care assistants can be employed to work in the client's own home. In England and Wales, most residential homes are in the private sector.

Voluntary care services

Voluntary care services are also non-statutory, but these are not run for profit. Many voluntary services are provided by charity organisations. The workers who provide the services can be paid or unpaid, or may have their expenses refunded. Some services are part of large organisations such as the NSPCC, while others may be small, local groups.

Voluntary care services cover a wide range of needs. Here are some examples:
+ Age Concern
+ Alcoholics Anonymous
+ Macmillan Cancer Relief
+ CRUSE Bereavement Care
+ MenCap
+ MIND
+ Relate
+ Riding for the Disabled
+ Samaritans
+ Women's Royal Voluntary Service

The typical organisation of a charitable voluntary organisation

ACTIVITY: Research the voluntary organisations that are working in your local community. Who do they help and what services do they provide?

Informal care services

Many individuals receive a great deal of care that is not provided by formal services. Family, friends and neighbours provide **informal care**. Informal care services provided by family and friends can include helping with personal hygiene tasks, shopping, cleaning, gardening and cooking meals.

AQA GCSE **Health & Social Care**

Informal care provided by family and friends can involve help with everyday tasks

It is estimated that over 5 million people provide unpaid care in England and Wales. Generally, more women than men are informal carers. Most people can expect to provide informal care at some point in their lives. While informal carers do not have the professional skills of paid workers, they are often able to supply care when professionals cannot – for example, they may be able to give time to the individual.

Obtaining care services and barriers to access

There are three ways to access care services. These are called methods of referral. **Self-referral** is when a person asks for the service. A **professional referral** involves a care worker arranging for a person to receive a service. For example, GPs sometimes refer their patients to hospital services; and social workers, having made an assessment of a client's needs, may refer him/her to services such as housing, day centres, lunch clubs and/or health services.

When a person is put in contact with a service by a relative, friend or neighbour, or any other person who is not a care worker, then this is called a **third-party referral**.

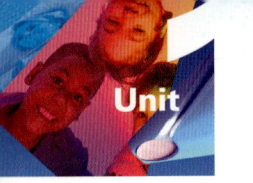

Unit

Health, social care & early years provision

Barriers to access

Sometimes people are unable to access care services easily. There can be many reasons for this. Anything that makes it difficult to access a service is called a barrier. Some examples of barriers to accessing services are shown in the diagram below.

Barriers to accessing services

It is important to overcome barriers to access in order for individuals to receive the care they need.

Physical barriers

Physical barriers, such as a lack of wheelchair facilities, can prevent access for individuals with physical disabilities. In this example, the barrier can be overcome by using a temporary ramp, which enables the wheelchair to ride over the steps. For individuals who cannot climb stairs, a lift may solve the problem.

Psychological barriers

Psychological barriers involve people's thoughts. For example, if an individual is afraid of being taken into a care home because he is elderly and cannot cope, he may not want to ask for help. Most elderly people value their independence and do not want to lose it. They feel that not

being able to look after themselves reduces their status and sense of self-worth.

Other individuals may fear the treatment that can result from accessing a care service. For example, the fear of having to go into hospital for an operation may prevent some individuals asking for help from their GP. For other individuals, it may be that they feel their problem is very personal and they may be too embarrassed to access the service. Generally, these psychological barriers can be overcome by giving information and reassurance. Talking through the person's fears will help.

Individuals with mental health conditions may find it difficult to understand the benefits that can be gained from accessing care. In these cases, specialist help may be needed to overcome the barrier.

Financial barriers

Financial barriers are about money. Care services that cost money can put people off accessing them — for example, dental services and chiropody. These barriers deter people who have low incomes or little money. Financial support is available for individuals in this situation — for example, help with NHS prescription charges, optical expenses and hospital travel costs. Information is again important, so that individuals know how to access this help.

Find out what financial help is available for people on low incomes.

Geographical barriers

Where a person lives in relation to where a service is based can be a barrier to access. People living in rural areas generally have to travel some distance to access some care services. This can be a problem if there is a lack of public transport and the person does not have a car. One way to overcome the problem is to have the service come into the remote rural area. For example, a GP might hold a local clinic one day each week.

Cultural and language barriers

Cultural beliefs about who should provide care and what should be done for the person can be a barrier (for example, Jehovah's witnesses will not accept blood transfusions). Problems with the English language can cause difficulties, whether or not English is the preferred language, and patients may not easily be able to describe their symptoms. In these cases, the use of a translator may help access, and talking

Definition

Cultural beliefs are the general customs or way of life of a particular group of people, usually based on their religious views and/or traditions.

Unit 1

Health, social care & early years provision

Research sign language and/or Braille. How do they work?

through the nature of care, respecting the individual's beliefs and views, can help.

Individuals who are deaf or have profound hearing difficulties may have problems accessing the care they need because they cannot make themselves understood, or do not understand what is being said to them. Individuals who are blind or have a severe visual impairment and those with speech problems may face similar problems. In these cases, other forms of communication, such as sign language and Braille, may be used.

Resource barriers

A lack of staff, information about services or money to fund services, or a heavy demand on the services from people who want to use them, can create barriers to access. These can be difficult to overcome because often there is no extra money available to provide more services. However, individuals do have choices as to where they access care services and they can lessen the problem by accessing care in another locality. Care managers monitor and schedule their services carefully to maximise the number of people they help. Initiatives like NHS Direct help to reduce the pressure on other NHS services.

Think of other examples of barriers to accessing care services. How might they may be overcome?

Job roles in health, social care and early years services

Care workers who deliver care directly to the client are called **direct care workers**. Care workers who are not so directly involved but still work to help the client are called **indirect care workers**.

To deliver effective care, all care workers must understand their client's needs. These can be obvious, for example when a person has broken a leg in a fall, or not so obvious, for example an elderly person living alone who has little contact with others and is therefore becoming socially isolated. Understanding the need is the starting point. Whatever the need, an assessment is usually carried out to determine what care actions should be taken.

Care workers rarely perform single care actions for clients. For example, a GP may diagnose illness, prescribe medicine, advise patients, refer patients to other services and monitor health, depending on the client's needs.

AQA GCSE **Health & Social Care**

Healthcare

GP

GPs take account of physical, psychological and social factors when diagnosing illness and recommending suitable treatment. They may also run specialist clinics within their practice for patients with specific conditions, such as diabetes. GPs will promote health education with other health professionals and organise preventative medical programmes for individual patients.

Some GPs specialise in certain areas of medicine such as **obstetrics**, **gynaecology**, **psychiatry** or **orthopaedics**.

What are the specialisms of GPs in your area?

> **Definitions**
>
> **Gynaecology** is the medical diagnosis and treatment of disorders of the female reproductive organs.
>
> **Obstetrics** is the medical care of women during pregnancy, childbirth and the period of recovery after childbirth.
>
> **Orthopaedics** is the medical and surgical care concerned with injuries to, and disorders of, the muscles and the skeleton.
>
> **Psychiatry** is the medical diagnosis, treatment and prevention of mental illness.

Nurse

Over 400 000 nurses are employed in the NHS in various roles.

Community/district nurse

Community/district nurses provide care to patients who are ill or not able to look after themselves, but who are not in hospital. The nursing care is usually given in the patient's own home, a residential care home or in a

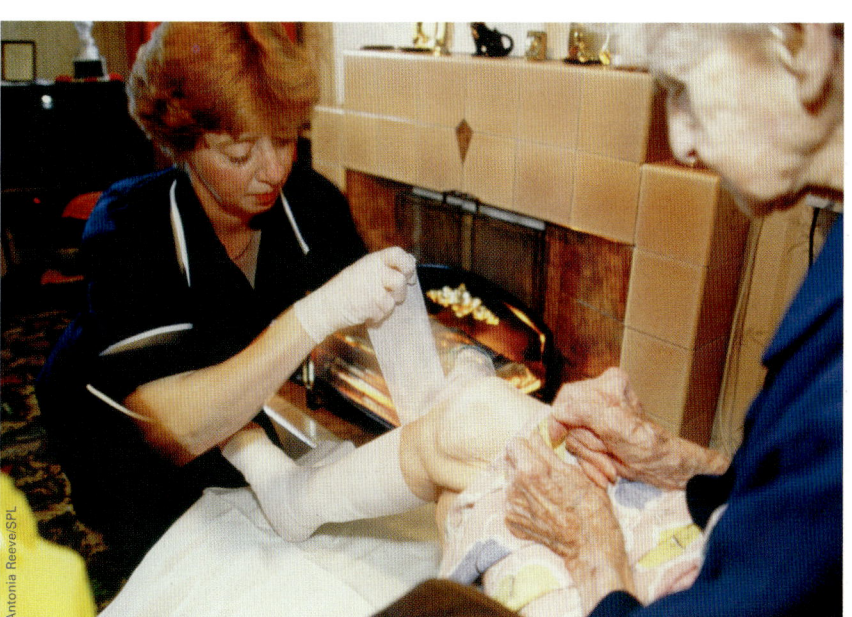

A district nurse bandaging the leg ulcer of an elderly client

19

Unit 1

Health, social care & early years provision

health centre. Patients needing care include those who are housebound, elderly, terminally ill and disabled, and people discharged recently from hospital.

Community/district nurses accept referrals from GPs and hospitals. They assess, plan and manage the care of patients. The nurses offer emotional support to patients and their families and carers and help them learn basic care-giving skills. This can include making sure that patients, families and carers understand the treatment and how medication should be given.

Common nursing tasks performed by community/district nurses are:

+ checking temperature, blood pressure and pulse
+ giving drugs and injections
+ cleaning and dressing wounds
+ taking blood and urine samples

Midwife

Midwives are specialist nurses. They have a range of responsibilities caring for mothers and their babies both during pregnancy and up to 28 days after birth. After this period, care is provided by a health visitor. Midwives diagnose, monitor and examine women during pregnancy, and assess, develop and evaluate individual programmes of care. They provide antenatal care, which includes screening tests, and provide counselling and advice. If problems such as miscarriage or stillbirth occur, midwives offer support and advice. During labour, when the child is being born, the midwife supervises and assists, monitoring the baby's condition and using his/her knowledge of drugs and pain management. After the birth, the midwife gives advice and support on breast feeding, bathing and making up feeds for the baby.

Health visitor

Health visitors are qualified nurses or midwives who are specially trained to assess health needs, promote good health and prevent illness by providing help and advice to individuals in the local community. They visit individuals in their homes, especially new mothers and children under 5 years of age. Health visitors also work with the elderly, with disabled people and with people with long-term illnesses.

The main roles of health visitors include:

+ listening, advising and supporting individuals on health and parenting needs — for example, feeding, safety, physical and emotional development, weaning and **immunisation**

> **Definition**
>
> **Immunisation** is the introduction of weak or dead forms of infectious disease organisms into the body to develop a person's immune system in order to protect against the disease in the future.

- delivering child health programmes
- managing parent and baby clinics
- delivering specialist clinics – for example, baby massage, exercise, child development and how to stop smoking
- identifying health needs in neighbourhoods – for example, health needs of the homeless
- providing health improvement programmes for individuals with specific needs – for example, sufferers with cancer or coronary heart disease
- counselling individuals on issues such as **post-natal depression**, bereavement or positive HIV diagnosis

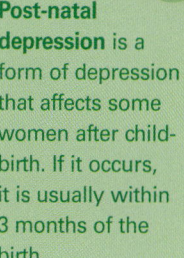

Definition

Post-natal depression is a form of depression that affects some women after child-birth. If it occurs, it is usually within 3 months of the birth.

Mental health nurse

Mental health nurses work with children, adults and the elderly who suffer from different forms of mental health problems. They may work in the client's own home, in residential care settings or in hospitals. Their main roles include:

- assessing and talking to parents about their problems
- reassuring patients about treatment
- building relationships and trust with patients
- listening to patients' concerns and interpreting their needs
- helping patients to manage their emotions and behaviour
- helping patients to develop social skills
- producing care plans and risk assessments for individual patients
- monitoring patient progress
- coordinating the care of patients

Practice nurse

Practice nurses work in GP practices. They provide nursing care to clients of all ages. Their main roles include:

- providing advice, information and consultations about minor ailments and health conditions
- performing minor operations and investigatory procedures – for example, ear syringing
- setting up and running certain clinics – for example, well-woman/man and asthma clinics
- giving contraceptive advice and fitting contraceptive devices
- performing cervical smears and pregnancy tests
- giving injections – for example, for infants and travellers
- offering first aid and emergency treatment if required
- recording notes of consultations and treatments in patients' files

Unit 1

Health, social care & early years provision

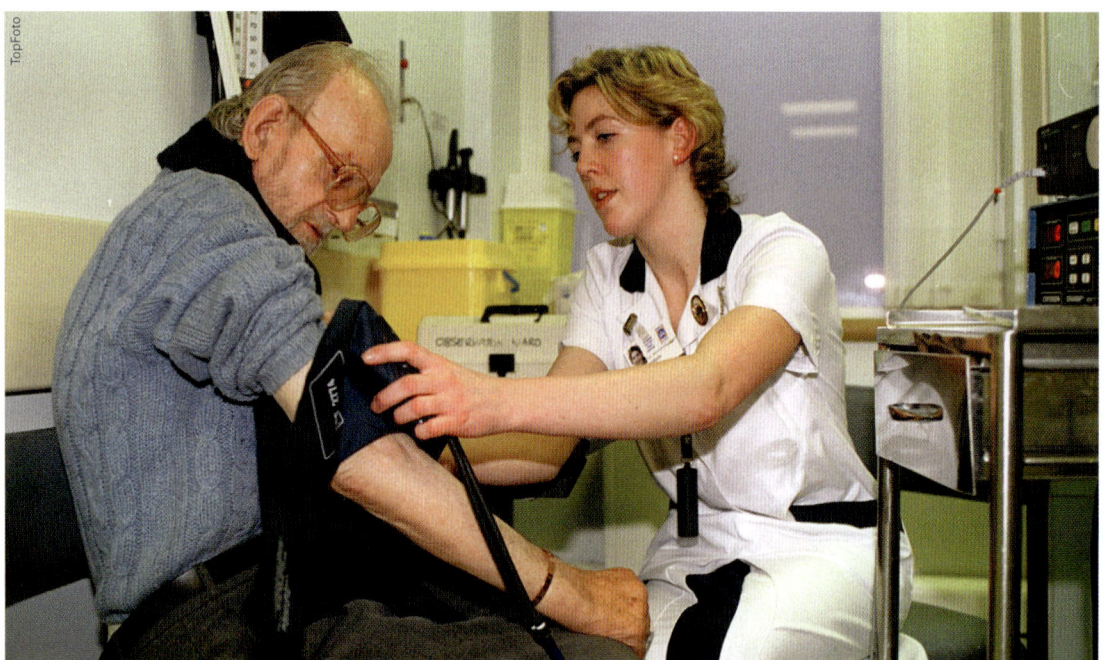

One of the tasks a nurse may have to perform is taking blood pressure

Other nursing roles

Some nurses work in hospital accident and emergency departments as triage officers. Their role is to sort casualties into order of priority for treatment. This is vital when the accident and emergency department is busy and may have large numbers of casualties to deal with – for example, after a multiple vehicle traffic accident. Triage officers assess each casualty in terms of ability to walk, respiratory rate and pulse rate. Decisions can then be made to prioritise patients. Some will require immediate treatment, while others may need urgent but not immediate attention. Treatment for some patients can be delayed while the more urgent and immediate cases are dealt with. It is vital that the most serious injuries are dealt with first as these can be life-threatening.

Some nurses specialise in children while others become adult nurses. Children's nurses are also called paediatric nurses. They work in hospital outpatient departments and other locations. They are experts in understanding the particular needs of children. Adult nurses provide medical care, promote good health and support the recovery of adult patients suffering from acute and long-term illness and diseases, and those requiring surgery. They work mainly in hospitals on general medical and surgical wards. They work in intensive care, operating theatres, recovery areas, accident and emergency departments and specialist clinics.

AQA GCSE **Health & Social Care**

Hospital doctor

Hospital doctors use their medical knowledge and skills to diagnose, prevent and treat illnesses, diseases and disorders in patients. They work in both NHS and private hospitals with inpatients in hospital wards and outpatients in clinics. Hospital doctors start as juniors. As they become specialists in a particular area of medicine or surgery, they become registrars or consultants.

Common specialist areas include:
+ anaesthetics (pain control using drugs)
+ cardiology (heart and blood vessels)
+ ophthalmology (eye diseases)
+ paediatrics (children's medical care)
+ pathology (study of disease)

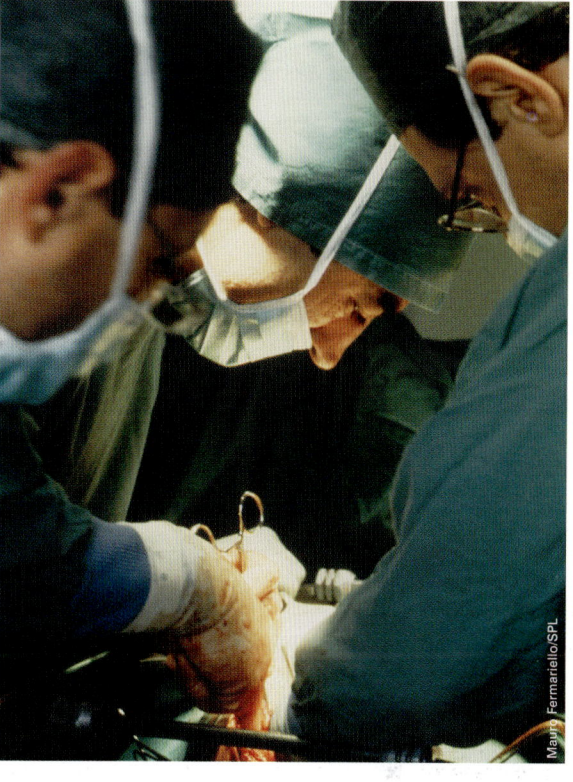

An operation in progress; hospital doctors can specialise in a particular area of surgery

The work they do depends on their specialist area. Generally, all hospital doctors will:
+ monitor and provide care to their patients
+ admit patients into hospital for specialist care investigations and treatment
+ diagnose medical conditions
+ keep records of treatment
+ refer patients back to GPs after treatment
+ work with other doctors and healthcare workers as part of a team

Occupational therapist

Occupational therapists (OTs) help individuals with physical, mental health or social problems to live as independently as possible. The problem may be present from birth or it could be caused by accident, operation, illness or ageing.

The typical roles of OTs include:
+ providing equipment or adaptations to help with daily living – for example, washing, preparing and eating meals, shopping and general mobility in and out of the home
+ helping with leisure and social activities
+ teaching coping skills such as relaxation techniques, positive thinking and assertiveness

Unit 1

Health, social care & early years provision

+ working with other healthcare professionals to plan and review treatment
+ organising support and rehabilitation groups for clients and their carers

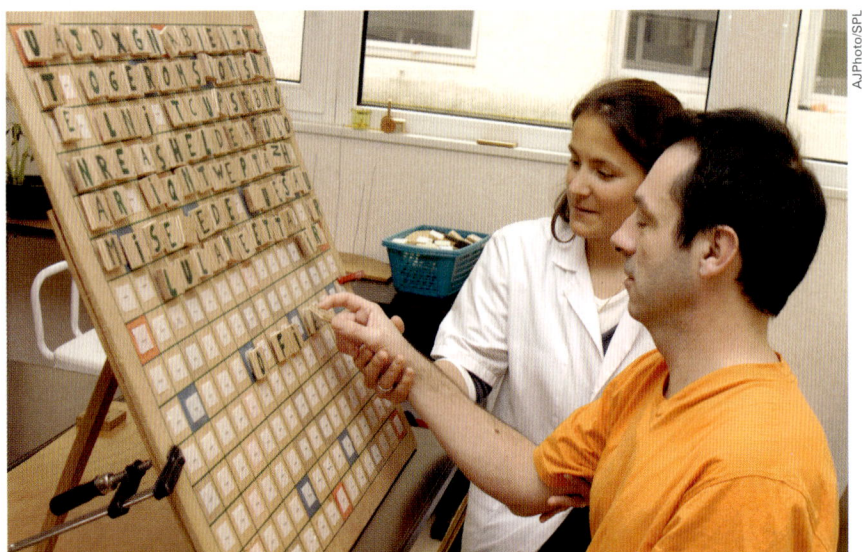

This occupational therapist is helping a stroke victim to make words on a board; the exercise will improve his coordination and muscle control

Definitions

Electrotherapy is the use of electrical energy to promote healing in injured tissue.

Hydrotherapy is exercising in water, which helps support weight while allowing movement.

Manual therapy means using hands to manipulate the limbs and joints of a patient, which enables him/her to maximise movement without pain.

Ultrasound is the use of sound waves above the upper limit of human hearing; when directed on the affected area they help movement by reducing inflammation and swellings.

Physiotherapist

Physiotherapists help people with physical problems caused by illness, injury, ageing or disability. These include individuals with sports injuries, stroke victims and the elderly whose joints and limbs have lost some ability to move easily. Physiotherapists use **manual therapy**, exercise movements and technological treatments. Examples include massage, manipulation, therapeutic movements, **ultrasound**, **electrotherapy** and **hydrotherapy**.

Radiographer

Radiographers work in hospitals and clinics. Most are diagnostic radiographers who use radioactive materials such as X-rays to produce images of parts of the body.

These are useful when investigating bones and problems in the digestive system. Some diagnostic radiographers use ultrasound for checking blood circulation, examining the heart and looking at babies developing in the womb.

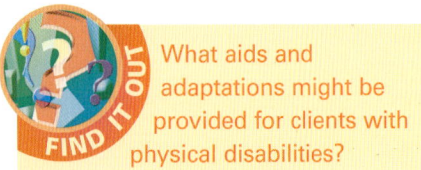

What aids and adaptations might be provided for clients with physical disabilities?

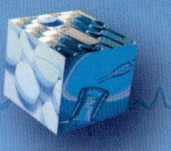

Some radiographers become therapeutic radiographers. These are sometimes called radiotherapy radiographers. Their main role is to work with doctors and nurses treating patients who have cancer. They give doses of X-rays and other radioactive materials to patients to kill or slow the growth of cancer cells in the body.

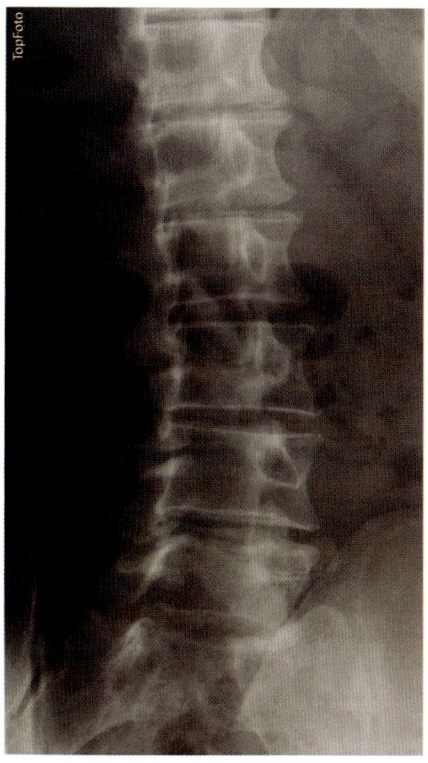

X-rays can be used to diagnose broken bones and other structural problems

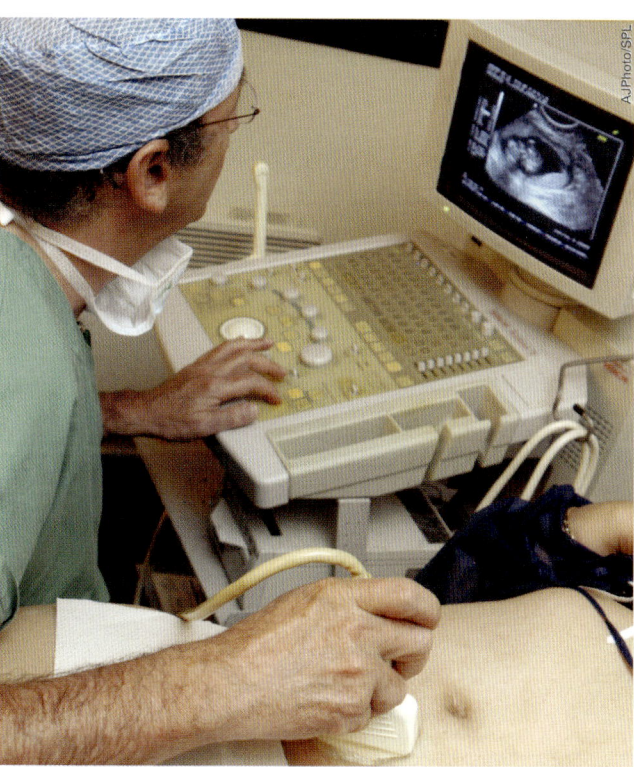

This radiographer is monitoring the growth of a developing baby in its mother's womb

Phlebotomist

Phlebotomists are specialist assistant healthcare scientists who collect blood from patients. The blood is then analysed in laboratories to give important information to help diagnose disease.

Phlebotomists have to be careful to take blood samples without harming the patient or disturbing the nursing care the patient may be receiving at the time. It is also important to take the blood correctly in case the sample is damaged and the resulting tests are either inaccurate or worthless. It is the phlebotomist's responsibility to transport the blood sample to the correct laboratory as and when needed.

Unit 1

Health, social care & early years provision

Pharmacist

Pharmacists are experts in the use of prescription and non-prescription medicines. Most pharmacists work in hospitals, community pharmacies or primary care pharmacies. Their main role is to make sure that patients get the maximum benefit from their medicines.

Pharmacists advise other healthcare staff on the selection and appropriate use of medicines. Pharmacists also help patients by providing information on how to manage their medicines to make sure they get appropriate treatment. They counsel and advise individuals on the treatment of minor health problems and on any side effects of the medicines. Pharmacists also advise people about possible interactions with other medicines and treatments the person may be receiving. Some pharmacists are qualified to prescribe medicines and may offer specialist health check services such as blood pressure monitoring, cholesterol level monitoring, pregnancy testing and diabetes screening.

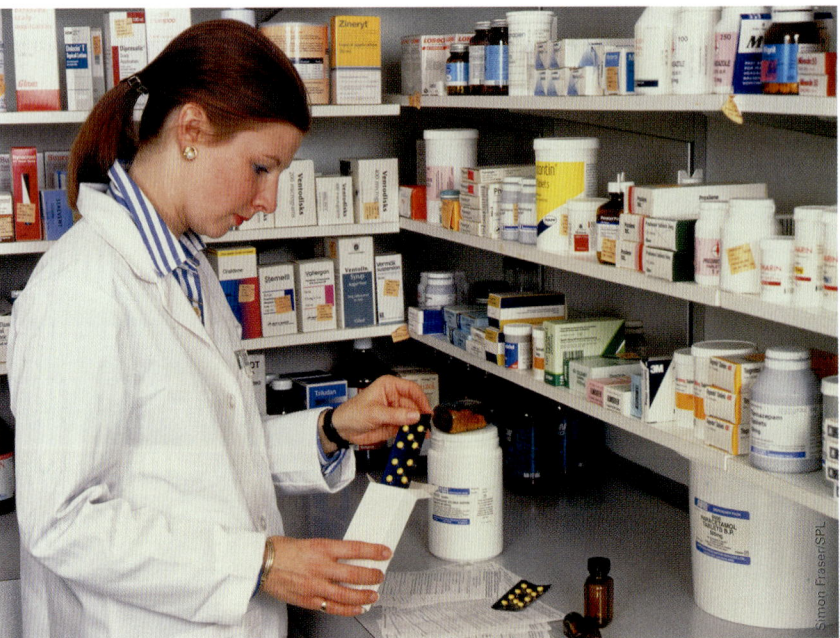

A pharmacist preparing a client's prescription for dispensing

Dentist/dental worker

Most dentists work in general practice, providing dental care to the public either under the NHS or, more commonly, as part of the private sector. The main roles include:

+ examining teeth and diagnosing dental problems

+ educating patients on good oral healthcare
+ carrying out agreed treatment – for example, providing fillings for teeth that have decayed
+ providing crowns and bridgework

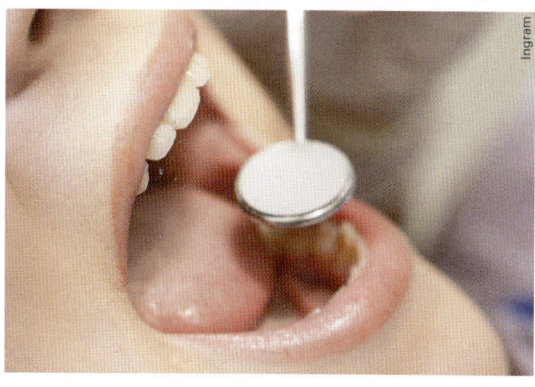

Dentists tend to work with other specialist staff such as dental nurses, dental hygienists and dental technicians. Dental nurses get appropriate instruments ready, mix filling materials, take notes from the dentist, make patients comfortable, tidy the surgery and sterilise all instruments. Dental hygienists remove hard and soft deposits from teeth, teach patients about good oral hygiene and provide other preventative dental care. They can also take dental X-rays and examine teeth and gums to record diseases or abnormalities. Dental technicians make dentures, crowns, bridges and dental braces.

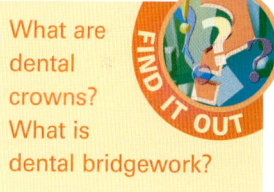

What are dental crowns? What is dental bridgework?

Optician

Opticians can be dispensing opticians or optometrists. Dispensing opticians fit glasses and contact lenses from prescriptions written by optometrists. Optometrists are sometimes called ophthalmic opticians. Their main role is to carry out eye examinations, checking the health of the eyes in order to produce a prescription for the patient. They carry out sight tests using specialist equipment and give advice on visual problems. Optometrists also check for signs and symptoms of certain health conditions that may be found when examining the eyes – for example, diabetes. If any are found, the patient is referred to a GP.

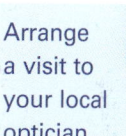

Arrange a visit to your local optician.

Audiologist

Audiologists work with patients to assess hearing and/or problems with balance. They recommend and provide appropriate rehabilitation to help. Audiologists work with patients of all ages, but most work is done with children and the elderly. This is because hearing problems are most common in these life stages. The audiologist's main roles include testing, treating and counselling patients and developing and improving hearing and balance test techniques.

Audiologists work alongside ear, nose and throat (ENT) specialist doctors, speech and language therapists, physiotherapists and teachers of the deaf in order to provide appropriate care.

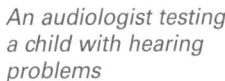

Health, social care & early years provision

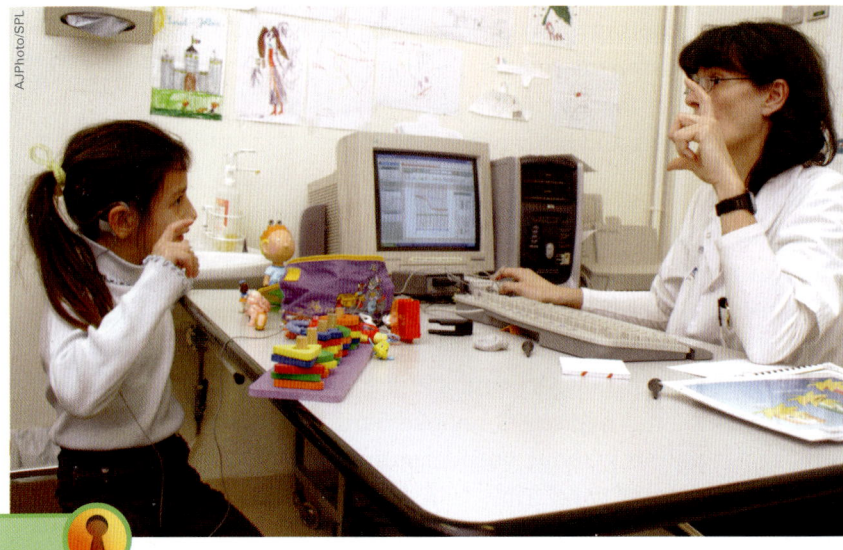

An audiologist testing a child with hearing problems

> **Definition**
>
> **Cleft palate** is a condition from birth when the two parts of the shell that make up the roof of the mouth do not completely join. It causes speech problems but can be treated by surgery.
>
> **Dementia** is a disorder affecting intellectual ability that involves loss of memory, judgement and abstract thinking skills. A person with dementia may also suffer from personality change as the condition develops.

Speech and language therapist

Speech and language therapists (SLTs) assess and treat speech, language and communication problems. They work with individuals of all ages, helping them to communicate effectively. They may also work with individuals who have problems swallowing and eating. Around 2.5 million people in the UK have a speech or language difficulty. Typical problems include stammering, difficulties understanding language and producing and using speech, and communication difficulties caused by strokes, hearing loss and deafness, **cleft palate**, **dementia** and head injuries.

Dietician

Dieticians produce practical dietary advice for individuals. To do this, they need to translate scientific information about foods into easily understood language for individuals who need normal or specialised diets. Dieticians promote a healthy, well-balanced diet, advise on food-related problems and treat disease and ill health. Many dieticians specialise with the NHS — for example, working with diabetics or cancer victims. Some dieticians work in the community and visit individuals at home.

Dieticians typically calculate the individual's nutritional requirements using assessments of blood chemistry, temperature, stress level, mobility and other relevant factors. They then suggest practical ways to improve well-being through healthier eating methods.

AQA GCSE **Health & Social Care**

A hospital dietician giving a client practical dietary advice

Other roles include advising hospital catering departments about specific dietary requirements of patients, and nursing clinics in hospital outpatient departments for individuals referred by GPs, health visitors or hospital consultants.

Chiropodist

Chiropodists are sometimes called podiatrists. They assess, diagnose and treat a range of problems of the feet and legs below the knees. They use their skills to treat minor infections, defects and injuries, such as **corns**, **calluses**, warts (**verrucae**), ulcers, in-growing nails and **bunions**.

Chiropodists treat problems of the feet and lower legs, such as bunions

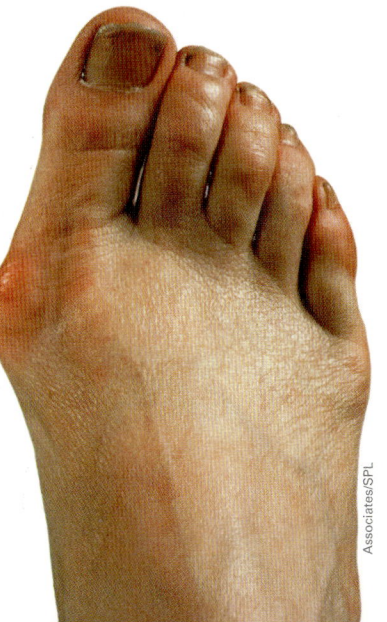

> ### Definitions
>
> **Bunions** are caused when the big toe is angled towards the second toe forming a bony lump on the side of the big toe. Tight shoes aggravate the condition, which is more common in women than men.
>
> **Calluses** are dead skin cells that harden and thicken. They are usually found on the ball of the foot, the heel and the inside of the big toe.
>
> **Corns** are calluses that form on the toes because bones push up against the shoe, putting pressure on the skin, which thickens and builds up.
>
> **Verrucae** are warts caused by a virus and are found on the soles of the feet or around the toes; they spread easily by direct contact in damp areas, e.g. swimming pool changing rooms or bathrooms.

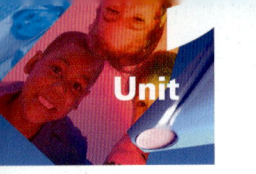

Unit

Health, social care & early years provision

Chiropodists use specialised dressings and exercise therapies, and perform minor surgery using local anaesthetics. They can prescribe and fit orthoses, which are inner sole inserts for footwear, to help mobility. Chiropodists also promote foot health by educating vulnerable individuals such as the homeless, the elderly, children and sufferers of arthritis.

Clinical psychologist

Clinical psychologists work with people of all ages who experience mental or physical health problems. These problems include:

- anxiety and depression
- mental illness
- adjusting to physical illness
- addiction
- eating disorders
- behaviour disorders
- relationship problems
- learning disabilities

Clinical psychologists aim to reduce distress and promote psychological well-being. Typically, they assess a client's needs, abilities or behaviour using interviews, tests and direct observation. They then produce and monitor appropriate programmes of treatment, such as therapy, counselling and advice. Many clinical psychologists specialise in work with one particular client group — for example, elderly adults, adults with mental health problems, child and family, or those with learning disabilities.

Nursing assistant

Nursing assistants are sometimes called healthcare assistants or auxiliary nurses. They have varied job roles in hospitals and community settings. Typically, they help with:

- washing and dressing
- feeding
- toileting
- bed making
- patient mobility
- obtaining urine, faeces and other samples
- routine urine analyses
- patient comfort

- monitoring of patients conditions (e.g. taking pulse and temperature, and measuring respiration and weight)
- ward cleanliness

They also provide support for the patient's family and friends. Some nursing assistants train to monitor blood pressure.

Social care

There are around 1.2 million social care workers in the UK. This is about 5% of the total UK workforce. Approximately 250 000 social care staff work in the NHS.

Social worker

Social workers often work with individuals who are socially excluded or experiencing some form of crisis in their lives. They provide support so that individuals can access services and help themselves. Their role can be as a critical friend, an **advocate** or a guide.

> **Definition**
> **Advocates** are those who can help people speak up for themselves so that their views are heard, their rights met and their problems sorted out.

Social workers provide support for a range of client groups with various problems

Health, social care & early years provision

Over 50% of social workers work with young people and their families. They may also work with people with mental health problems, young offenders, school non-attenders, drug and alcohol abusers, people with learning disabilities, people with physical disabilities and the elderly. They work in day care, education, healthcare, mental health and residential settings.

Social workers assess their clients' needs. The initial assessment might be done immediately in emergency situations or usually within 7 days in other circumstances.

Interviews are conducted with clients and their families in order to assess and review the situation. The assessments are then written up. Information and counselling support can be offered to both the client and the family. Packages of support are organised and managed to allow clients to live the fullest lives possible. This may mean working with a range of service providers. The care services provided for clients are monitored over time.

Residential social workers are also known as residential support workers or care officers. They work in care homes, children's homes, hostels, and youth and adult centres with vulnerable clients. They work alongside qualified social workers.

Generally, residential social workers work in one of three main client groups — children and young people, adults or elderly people. For children and young people, they act as positive role models. They assess the needs of the child and establish good behaviour guidelines. They provide emotional and social support. As the child grows up and is about to leave formal care, they offer advice on independent living.

For adults, the residential social workers help with daily living skills (social and personal). This often involves participation in community and leisure activities.

For the elderly group, they check that the individuals are safe, comfortable and in a stimulating environment, and that they are treated with dignity.

All residential social care workers help to devise and carry out care plans agreed with the resident, his/her family and other care workers.

Home care assistant

Home care assistants give practical help with daily living activities to people in their own homes. This may involve working with elderly people, children, families or individuals with physical or learning disabilities. The main roles of home care assistants include personal care, such as dressing, toileting, washing and feeding, and providing emotional and social support. Home care assistants may also help people with letter writing or organising their finances — for example, paying bills or budgeting.

Counsellor

Counsellors work in private and confidential settings with individual clients. A counsellor's main role is to explore with the clients the difficulties they may experience and the feelings of distress or dissatisfaction they have in life. The counsellor listens to the clients and encourages them to think clearly about their situation. Counsellors do not give advice or suggest answers to the clients, but aim to help them choose what to do. The counsellor aims to promote understanding by reducing confusion.

A counsellor's role typically includes establishing a trusting relationship with each client. This involves respecting the clients, listening, helping them think clearly with new perspective, accepting the clients' views without bias, helping them make choices and decisions, and referring them to other sources of help.

Counselling is only done with the consent of the client. Some counsellors specialise in particular areas — for example, marriage guidance, sexual abuse, drug abuse or health work.

Home care assistants provide practical help with daily living activities

Early years care

Early years care is for children from birth up to 8 years of age. Here are some of the early years direct care roles.

Nursery nurse

Nursery nurses work in schools, local authority nurseries, private nurseries, family centres and hospitals. Some nursery nurses work in private homes as nannies. Their main roles include:
+ helping young children learn through play, so they develop educationally and socially

Unit 1

Health, social care & early years provision

A nursery nurse playing with young children in the classroom

Painting is a popular pastime with young children

- helping to feed, wash and clean the children
- observing and monitoring children and keeping appropriate records
- supporting other workers involved with young children, such as social workers and healthcare staff, in making and maintaining learning resources

THINK ABOUT IT — What play activities might help young children to learn?

Most nursery nurses work with healthy children, but some specialise in working with children with health problems. Nursery nurses may work with physically disabled children or those with learning difficulties.

Senior nursery nurses may become nursery supervisors, taking on management roles.

Nursery assistant

Nursery assistants often work with nursery nurses and others in early years care settings. They help the nursery nurse plan and prepare activities and supervise care for the young children at all times. They also help keep appropriate records and make sure that playrooms and equipment are clean and maintained ready for use.

Playgroup leader

Playgroup leaders plan, organise and supervise play activities for children. They aim to help children participate in imaginative play, sports, music, dance, outdoor activities, cooking and creativity. Playgroup leaders generally work in community or private preschool settings. They supervise staff, plan programmes of activities and report to the playgroup committee, chairperson or owner. They are usually aided by playgroup assistants.

Childminder

Childminders are professional carers who work in their own homes providing care and learning opportunities for other people's children. There are nearly 80 000 childminders in England and Wales looking after more than 300 000 children.

All childminders have to be registered by law. Their homes are inspected to make sure they are safe and suitable places for children. Childminders must be trained in first aid and have to be insured in case accidents occur or the child they are looking after damages someone else's property.

Generally, childminders are registered to look after up to three children under the age of 5 years and three children between the ages of 5 and 8 years, in addition to their own children. They may also look after older children.

Some childminders take on extra training to work with disabled children and those with other special needs.

Early years teacher

Early years teachers/nursery teachers work with 3–5 year olds, aiming to help them progress smoothly into primary schools. They develop schemes of work and lesson plans and organise the learning environment and resources to help learning. They aim to foster enthusiasm for learning, using visual aids and other teaching resources. Early years teachers share knowledge gained with other nursery workers and the parents of the children. It is important that they observe, assess and record the development of the young children in their care.

Some early years nursery teachers visit each child's home before he/she starts at the nursery.

Unit 1: Health, social care & early years provision

A pre-school teacher reading aloud to her class

Classroom assistant

Early years teachers are usually aided by a classroom assistant. Classroom assistants may also be found in primary and special educational schools. They are sometimes called teaching assistants or teaching associates. They are an extra pair of hands in the classroom, often working one to one with pupils. The classroom assistants' role typically includes helping to photocopy materials, collect dinner money and prepare equipment.

Learning support assistant

Learning support assistants work with children who have special needs and/or disabilities. They generally work with particular children individually or in small groups, providing close support and help. Like other classroom assistants, they prepare materials for the children and promote self-help and the development of social skills. They support the teacher in the classroom with the delivery of lessons. This might include helping with basic arithmetic and reading, encouraging pupils to interact appropriately, collecting work and overseeing activities.

Indirect care worker

Direct care workers and their clients need the support of indirect care workers in order to meet the needs of individuals. Table 1 shows a variety of indirect care jobs and their main roles and responsibilities.

Job	Care role
Hospital hotel services manager	Management responsibilities for accommodation, catering, cleaning, laundry, portering, security, transport and waste disposal
Hospital porter	Moving patients, laundry, furniture and equipment; delivering post; disposing of waste
Dental receptionist	Maintaining smooth running of reception area; operating switchboard; welcoming visitors/clients; handling mail
Medical secretary	Supporting GPs/consultants; answering telephone; maintaining files/word-processing notes
Residential home catering officer	Ordering foodstuffs; organising catering staff; devising menus; maintaining hygiene standards and meeting health and safety requirements
Medical receptionist	Greeting patients; filing medical records; arranging appointments; dealing with mail; dealing with requests
GP practice manager	Dealing with accounts, records, business strategy and recruitment; training/supervising staff
Health records clerk	Checking medical records; opening, maintaining, filing and retrieving
Ambulance driver	Driving to emergency calls; providing non-urgent transport for patients
Cleaner	Removing litter and grime from the building, making it safe and pleasant to be in

Table 1 Indirect care workers

The value bases of care work

All care workers aim to help people live as independently as possible. For some individuals, a lot of care is required, which may involve specialist healthcare on the one hand and help with daily living tasks on the other. No matter what care is given, all care workers understand the values that are essential features of all care. We call these the **value bases of care**. Care workers often have their own names for them. The value bases of care are sometimes written into the charters and codes of practice that apply to particular jobs, or they might be found in the rules or guidelines that the workers follow. They may be found in care setting policies, procedures or employment contracts. In some cases, they are not written down at all, but the care workers know they exist because of what is expected of them and how they are trained. In some cases, they are used to check the quality of care.

Health, social care & early years provision

Promoting anti-discriminatory practice

Individuals need to be treated fairly by healthcare, social care and early years care workers. This means they must be treated according to their individual needs. Because everyone is different and has different needs, we should not all be treated the same. For example, by treating people according to their needs, they will be treated fairly by care workers regardless of their gender, race, culture, social background, sexuality or disability.

Therefore, treating individuals equally is not always appropriate. Everyone should have their needs met — that is both fair and equal. This means, however, that some individuals need more time and resources than others. In this sense, the care given is not equal.

Maintaining confidentiality of information

It is important that care workers maintain the confidentiality of information relating to their clients. This does not mean that all information is kept secret from everyone. Where care workers work with others, there is a need to share relevant information so that effective care can be given. However, care workers should not discuss their client's details — for example, medical conditions or personal circumstances — with any other individuals without the consent of the client.

Where written records are made, these should be kept securely under lock and key. Computerised client records need password protection. Permission should always be obtained from the client before sharing information and the client should always know the reasons why the information needs to be shared.

Information about clients must be kept confidential

Under certain circumstances, a client's right to confidentiality has to be limited — for example, if they are unable to give this information themselves, or if they are a danger to themselves or other people. There are principles laid down for how all health and social care workers should treat client information. We shall look at these later in this chapter.

> **THINK ABOUT IT**
> Under what circumstances would a client be unable to give permission for the sharing of personal information?

Promoting and supporting an individual's rights to dignity, independence, health and safety

Care workers need to promote and support their client's rights to dignity by treating them with respect. Clients who need the help of care workers often feel vulnerable, anxious or fearful. Control of their care is in the hands of the carers rather than themselves. The client may feel a loss of **dignity** if tasks have to be done for them that they would normally do themselves, such as feeding and washing. Good care practice aims to prevent loss of dignity. For example, care workers should do all they can to maintain the client's privacy. They should address their clients appropriately at all times and not become over-familiar with them.

A client's right to dignity is supported if he/she is able to act as independently as possible. By allowing clients to make their own choices and decisions, care workers empower their clients. If care workers do not encourage the clients to act for themselves, the clients will become over-dependent on the carers. This leads to a loss of **independence** and a probable further loss of dignity.

The **health and safety** of clients is the first concern of all care workers. It governs all aspects of a carer's work — for example, monitoring clients' medical conditions, controlling medicine taken and preventing accidents.

> **ACTIVITY**
> Choose three different types of care worker. For each one, suggest two different ways in which they can help maintain client health and safety.

Acknowledging individual personal beliefs and identity

Care workers need to treat all clients as individuals. Everyone is different and is entitled to his/her own **personal beliefs**. Our culture, upbringing, religion and views make us who we are. If care workers did not treat their clients as individuals, they would make assumptions or judgements about them based on, for example, how they look. This would mean the care workers stereotyping the clients and making each one fit a group image. This could lead to the client not receiving the care that he/she needs, or receiving inappropriate care. For example, if a person chooses to be a Jehovah's Witness, his/her beliefs may affect the medical care required. Jehovah's Witnesses do not accept blood transfusions. Respecting personal beliefs is therefore important as it both empowers the client and helps to provide individualised care.

Protecting individuals from abuse

Abuse can be physical, sexual or emotional (sometimes called psychological abuse) or can involve neglect. Everybody has the right not to be abused in any way. Individuals in need of care are not always able to protect themselves from abuse. For example, elderly individuals who are easily confused may be vulnerable to dishonest people who can take advantage of the situation. This can be through theft of money or personal possessions from their homes, or overcharging for non-essential home repairs. Instances like these cause great distress to the elderly victims, damaging both their emotional and physical health and well-being. Children are another client group that may be vulnerable to different forms of abuse by adults.

Not providing appropriate care is neglect. It is the responsibility of all carers to protect those in their care. This is best done by monitoring and observing the clients carefully. Establishing trust between carer and client helps the sharing of information between the two, and will alert the carer if anything untoward is happening.

Providing individualised care

Individuals may have identical care needs but that does not mean that the care they receive should be identical. As we have said already, care workers need to take into account the individual client's personal beliefs and rights to choose the care that is appropriate for each case. For example, elderly clients who find it difficult to cope by themselves at home may want the help of a home care assistant to help with everyday living tasks in the house. These clients may want to protect their independence for as long as possible. Other elderly clients in the same circumstances may be less concerned about their independence in this way and may feel that a residential home is a more appropriate option for them. They would have

A home care assistant helping an elderly client to dress

the reassurance of constant care support. Whatever health, social or early years care is given, it should always be appropriate to meet the needs of the individual client's circumstances.

Effective communication

Getting the language right is essential for good carer–client relationships. Carers show respect by addressing clients appropriately and using a suitable level of language. On the one hand, the level of language should be not so technical that the client does not understand, but on the other hand not so simple that the client feels that he/she is being 'talked down to'. Tone of voice is also important, as is volume. A harsh tone of voice may cause a vulnerable client to be fearful of the carer. If the carer speaks too quietly, the client may not hear; too loud and he/she may feel shouted at. It is not always easy to get it right. Care workers need to be good listeners and observers as well as talkers.

It is important to remember that effective communication is a two-way process between the carer and the client.

Non-verbal language, sometimes called **body language**, is also important. Care workers use facial expressions such as smiling and head nodding to reassure clients. They make appropriate eye contact and stand or sit in a non-threatening way. This often means with an open, rather than a

Unit 1

Health, social care & early years provision

closed, stance, that is, 'square on' to the client rather than 'side on', and at an appropriate distance. Too close, and the client's personal space is invaded; too far away and the client may feel cut off. Carers often lean forward when sitting near the client. This is one way to show interest. Something as simple as holding the hand of an injured or distressed client can be reassuring and help to calm the client.

Effective communication is a two-way process between carer and client

The value bases of care and what they mean

Value bases of care:
- Promoting effective communication and relationships
- Promoting anti-discriminatory practice
- Maintaining confidentiality of information
- Providing individualised care
- Promoting and supporting an individual's rights to dignity, independence, health and safety
- Protecting individuals from abuse
- Acknowledging individual personal beliefs and identity

ACTIVITY: Role play a carer–client conversation, first using poor body language and then using good body language.

All the value bases underpin every care action given to help meet a need, whether it be a health need, a social care need or an educational need in the case of early years individuals.

Whatever they are called and whether written down or not, it is important to remember that *all* the value bases of care apply *all* the time. When looking at a single care action performed by a care worker, only some of the bases may be obvious, but all are still there.

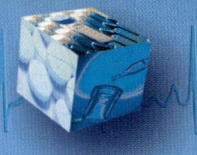

For example, Mr Jones is an elderly and frail patient who cannot bathe himself. John, a nurse, helps him.

The most obvious value bases underpinning this action are supporting Mr Jones's right to dignity, health and safety. John would do this by ensuring privacy for Mr Jones in the bathroom and checking the water temperature, so that Mr Jones is not scalded or chilled. Less obvious, but still just as important are the other value bases (Table 2).

Table 2 Caring for Mr Jones

Part of care action	Value base
By bathing Mr Jones when he needs it and not leaving him until other residents are bathed	John prevents **discrimination** against Mr Jones by treating him fairly according to his needs
By not talking about Mr Jones's health or frailty to other people not involved in his care	John maintains the **confidentiality** of information about Mr Jones
By letting Mr Jones do as much as he can to bathe himself	John promotes Mr Jones's **independence**; this empowers Mr Jones and maintains his self-esteem and self-confidence
By showing respect for Mr Jones's privacy while helping him bathe	John respects Mr Jones's dignity
By taking care to help Mr Jones to bathe safely in privacy	John protects Mr Jones from abuse by others
By using appropriate language and body language when bathing Mr Jones	John promotes **effective communication** between them and builds trust in the **relationship** between him and Mr Jones
By bathing Mr Jones carefully, helping him only as needed but not when he can do it himself	John provides individualised care appropriate for Mr Jones and is acknowledging that he is an individual with his own **identity**

Any care action can be looked at in this way to show *all* parts of the value base underpinning the care.

THINK ABOUT IT
When a GP sees a patient in the surgery, how does the value base underpin the consultation and care given?

Nurses need to build trust in their relationship with their patients

Health, social care & early years provision

Codes of practice, policies and procedures

All care workers are trained to understand the importance of what they do and to work appropriately at all times. There are many different forms of the rules, guidelines, policies and practices based on the value bases of care, which set out how different care workers should act. For example, the six **Caldicott principles** set out how workers in health and social care organisations should treat client information. The principles are as follows:

1 Justify the purpose(s).
2 Do not use personally identifiable information unless it is absolutely necessary.
3 Use the minimum personally identifiable information.
4 Access to personally identifiable information should be on a strict need-to-know basis.
5 Everyone should be aware of his/her responsibilities.
6 Understand and comply with the law.

Following these principles ensures that client confidentiality is maintained.

Although care jobs may be different, the codes or principles are often similar. All nurses, midwives and health visitors work with the **Nursing Midwifery Council** (NMC) *Code of Professional Conduct.* Here is a summary of the code:

> As a registered nurse, midwife or specialist community public health nurse you must:
> + respect the patient or client as an individual
> + obtain consent before you give any treatment or care
> + cooperate with others in the team
> + protect confidential information
> + monitor your professional knowledge and competence
> + be trustworthy
> + act to identify and minimise the risk to patients and clients

Social workers are governed by the General Social Care Council. This is a summary of their code of practice:

AQA GCSE **Health & Social Care**

As a social worker you must:
+ protect the rights and promote the interests of service users and carers
+ strive to establish and maintain the trust and confidence of service users and carers
+ promote the independence of service users while protecting them as far as possible from danger or harm
+ respect the rights of service users while seeking to ensure that their behaviour does not harm themselves or other people
+ uphold public trust and confidence in social care services
+ be accountable for the quality of your work and take responsibility for maintaining and improving your knowledge and skills

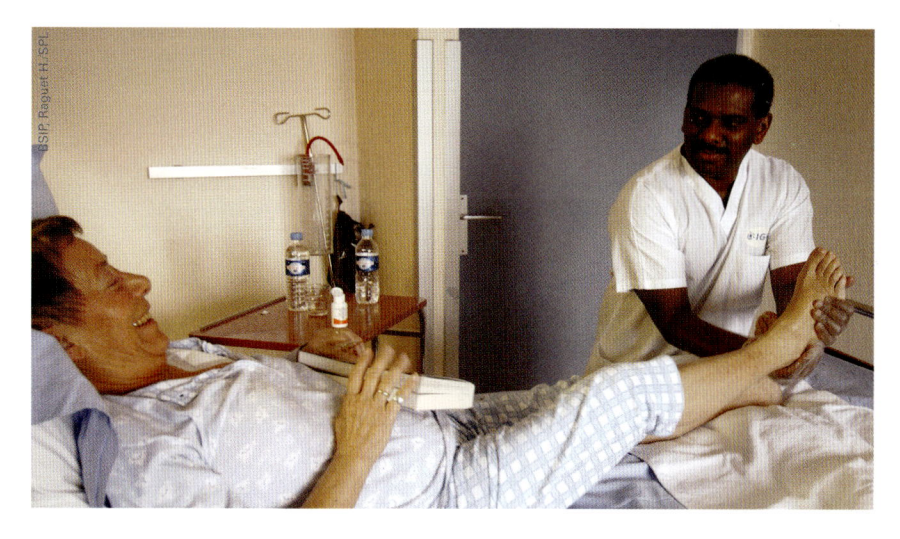

Registered nurses must follow the NMC Code of Professional Conduct.

Doctors are registered with the **General Medical Council**. The council has produced guidelines for doctors in a document called *Good Medical Practice*. This sets out the principles and values for doctors to follow. It also lets the public know what they can expect from doctors. Here is a copy of the guidelines:

Patients must be able to trust doctors with their lives and health. To justify that trust you must show respect for human life and you must:
+ make the care of your patient your first concern
+ protect and promote the health of patients and the public

45

Health, social care & early years provision

> - **+ provide a good standard of practice and care**
>   - keep your professional knowledge and skills up to date
>   - recognise and work within the limits of your competence
>   - work with colleagues in ways that best serve patients' interests
> - **+ treat patients as individuals and respect their dignity**
>   - treat patients politely and considerately
>   - respect patients' right to confidentiality
> - **+ work in partnership with patients**
>   - listen to patients and respond to their concerns and preferences
>   - give patients the information they want or need in a way they can understand
>   - respect patients' right to reach decisions with you about their treatment and care
>   - support patients in caring for themselves to improve and maintain their health
> - **+ be honest and open and act with integrity**
>   - act without delay if you have good reason to believe that you or a colleague may be putting patients at risk
>   - never discriminate unfairly against patients or colleagues
>   - never abuse your patients' trust in you or the public's trust in the profession
>
> You are personally accountable for your professional practice and must always be prepared to justify your decisions and actions.

While the words may be different, the aims of the Nursing Midwifery Council *Code of Professional Conduct*, the General Social Care Council *Code of Practice* and the doctors' *Good Medical Practice* guidelines are all similar.

You will notice that whatever the code, charter, set of rules or guidelines used in health and social care, they are there to ensure the quality of care. They put the value bases of care into action for their particular job roles. Much of the training of care workers focuses on quality of provision, value bases and codes of conduct.

The assessment requirements

You need to produce portfolio work on how the needs of two individuals from two different client groups may be met by service providers in your local area. You must include in your work:

AQA GCSE **Health & Social Care**

- the organisation of the services and the roles of people who work in them to meet the needs of your two chosen individuals
- how the care value base underpins work in supporting the two individuals
- relevant codes of practice or charters
- ways in which different types of communication skills are used to support your chosen individuals

You must work independently on your portfolio. Group work is not allowed. All the work must be yours. If you use any information from books or websites, make sure you say so. This is done using referencing and a bibliography. Remember that two individuals from the same age groups can be chosen if one of them has a disability. Start with some basic details about the individuals. Remember, it is important to maintain confidentiality — refer to them as Mr X or Mrs Y or any name you choose.

Write about the two individuals' needs first. Then work through the bullet points above in order.

Read through the checklist of 'dos and don'ts' in Table 3 to make sure you get it right.

You must work independently on your portfolio

47

Health, social care & early years provision

Building a good Unit 1 portfolio

Table 3 lists some important dos and don'ts you need to consider if you want high marks for your portfolio assessment. Follow the list for success.

Table 3
Getting it right

Dos	Don'ts
+ Choose two individuals from different client groups	+ Don't choose only one client, or two from the same group
+ Write about the clients' needs — health, social and/or educational, perhaps using PIES (physical, intellectual, emotional and social) analyses	+ Don't write about services provided as though they are needs, e.g. 'he needs an optician' (the need is for treatment of the eye problem)
+ Research actual local provision	+ Don't copy out of textbooks — even this one
+ Write about the organisation of local services — how they fit the national framework and how they are organised 'internally'; a diagram may help	+ Don't draw on 'general' diagrams without naming local services and structures; include services not used by clients; miss out information on internal structure relevant to the client's care; or write about only one care worker per client
+ Write about three or four care workers for each chosen client; include details of care actions performed for each client	+ Don't write vaguely or generally about care (e.g. 'the GP cares for client X') or include irrelevant information on care roles (e.g. salaries, wages, training, qualifications, hours worked)
+ Analyse the care actions, linking them to the different value bases of care; make sure you use all the value bases	+ Don't write general explanations of the care value bases or just link one value base to a care action
+ Select and include relevant parts of codes, charters, rules or guidelines (written or not) and show how these link to the care actions	+ Don't include complete copies or even parts of codes, charters, rules, guidelines etc. as downloaded/textbook information, if they are not linked by you to core actions
+ Write about verbal and non-verbal (body language) communication used by care workers when delivering the named care actions	+ Don't write generally about communication; include pages of facial expressions; or write about the client's use of communication
+ Keep the work in the bullet point order of Section 8.3 of the specification, using section headings to keep it clear	+ Don't mix up different sections of work and write it out in one piece with no clear indication of what each part is

Unit 2

Promoting health and well-being

Unit 2

Promoting health and well-being

This unit covers:
+ definitions of health and well-being
+ common factors that affect health and well-being and the different effects they can have on individuals and groups across the lifespan
+ methods used to measure an individual's physical health
+ ways of promoting and supporting health improvement for an individual or small group

You need to learn:
+ what health and well-being is
+ what factors contribute positively to health and well-being throughout the lifespan
+ what factors are a risk to health and well-being and how they can have a damaging effect
+ how an individual's physical health can be measured
+ how an individual can be motivated and supported to improve his/her health

What is health and well-being?

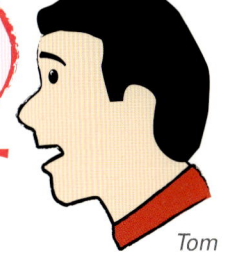

We all have different thoughts about what being healthy and well means.

Tom's idea is called a **negative definition**. This does not mean it is a bad idea; simply that by not having an illness, disease or something wrong, we might think that we are healthy and well.

I'm healthy because there's nothing wrong with me

Tom

Unit 2

Promoting health and well-being

Dick: I'm healthy because I'm really fit

Dick's idea can be seen as the opposite of Tom's. It is called a **positive definition**. Again, this does not mean it is good (or better than Tom's negative definition). It just means that to have fitness of body, and mind for that matter, is another way of looking at health and well-being.

Harry: I'm healthy because I have good physical, intellectual, emotional and social well-being

Harry's view is different again. This is called the **holistic view** because it takes in **p**hysical, **i**ntellectual, **e**motional and **s**ocial aspects (PIES). With all four of these being good, Harry believes he is healthy and well.

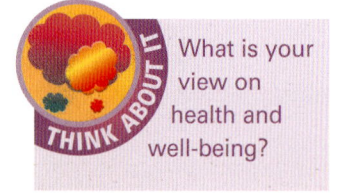

Tom, Dick and Harry have different views but none is right or wrong. People just see health and well-being differently.

Individuals' views about health and well-being can change over time. How you view health and well-being may be shaped by your culture and upbringing. Your views on factors and risks affecting health and well-being may also be affected by these.

THINK ABOUT IT — What is your view on health and well-being?

Positive factors affecting health and well-being

A major factor affecting our health and well-being is **food**.

Balanced diet

We need a balanced diet to stay healthy. This means eating the right amounts of different foods for our age and activity level. When we are growing rapidly or very active, we need more food than when we are not growing or less active. Our body size also determines how much food we eat — the bigger the person, the more food is needed.

Whatever the amount, having a balanced diet also means having the right balance of the different **components** in our food and drink.

The major food components that make up most of the foods we eat are called **macronutrients**. There are three main food component groups:
+ carbohydrates
+ fats
+ proteins

52

Carbohydrates

Carbohydrates are found in two forms — **sugars** and **starches**. Naturally formed foods that taste sweet contain sugars of some kind — for example, fruits such as plums and apples and vegetables such as carrots and beetroot. Food manufacturers often add sugar to make their products taste sweet. This means that people who eat a lot of chocolate, sweets and non-diet fizzy drinks take in far more sugar in the diet than they need.

Starches are found in foods such as rice, potatoes, bread and pasta. Starches are not sweet-tasting.

All carbohydrates give us energy to move around and keep us warm.

Sugars are broken down quickly to release energy. Starches are bigger, more complex molecules that take longer to break down. Starches are first changed to sugars before releasing their energy in the body tissues.

Most of the energy we need to stay alive, keep warm and move comes from carbohydrates in our diets.

> **ACTIVITY**
> Try chewing a piece of bread and not swallowing it. As the starch in the bread slowly changes into sugars, it will start to taste sweet.

Carbohydrates in our diet give us the energy we need for exercise

Unit 2: Promoting health and well-being

Fats

People trying to lose weight often think that fats are bad food components. This is not true, as fats are essential for a balanced diet and good health and well-being. Fats can supply us with energy and act as energy stores. They surround and protect organs of the body, like the kidney, and help keep heat in the body by acting as an insulation layer under the skin.

Different types of fat are found in different foods, such as meat, butter, milk, nuts, cakes and biscuits. Oils such as olive oil and sunflower oil are liquid fats. Some types of fat can be very harmful if eaten in too large a quantity. These are called saturated fats, and come from animal foodstuffs.

The fat content of some foods is affected greatly by the way the food is cooked. For example, frying in lard (an animal fat) increases the saturated fat content of the food. Grilling or steaming the food adds no fat. If the fat content increases, so does the energy content of the food. For example, a rasher of streaky bacon typically contains 400 kcal (1670 kJ) of energy if grilled. If it is fried in fat, the energy content rises to 500 kcal (2090 kJ). Frying causes the rasher of bacon to gain around 5 grams of fat.

Proteins

Proteins are needed for growth, repair and maintenance of the body tissues. They are found in many foods, including meat, fish, eggs, cheese, milk, peas, beans and lentils. Our bodies do not normally use protein for energy supply, but if insufficient carbohydrate or fat is available, protein can be used.

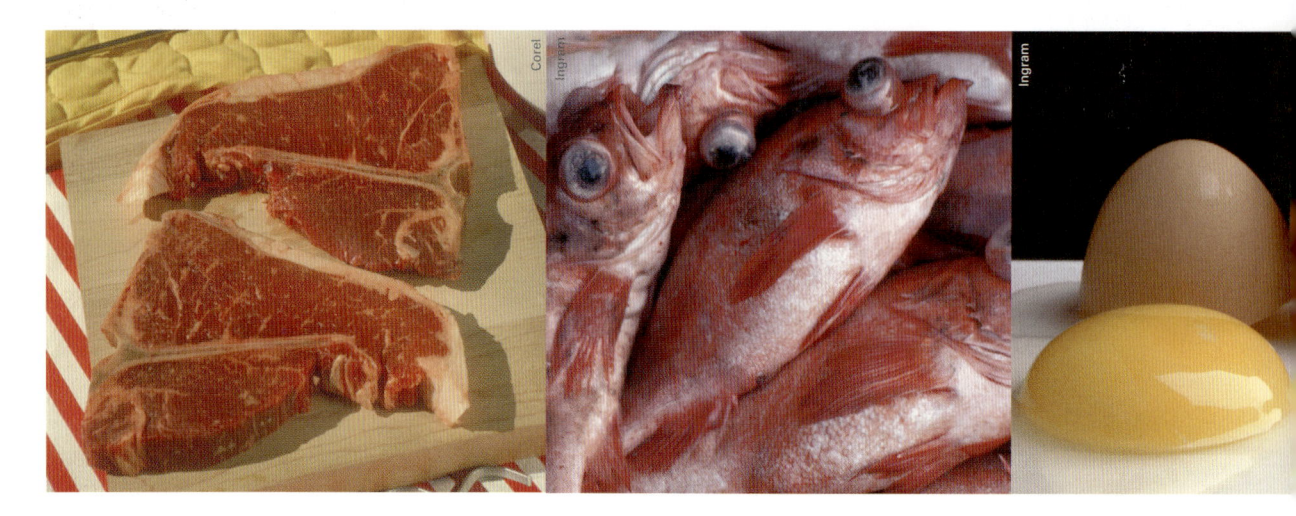

AQA GCSE **Health & Social Care**

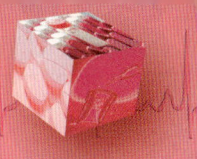

Proteins are found in meat, fish, eggs, milk, cheese, nuts, peas and beans; they are essential for building healthy bones and for the maintenance of body tissues. The addition of fresh fruits and vegetables to the diet provides essential carbohydrates and a rich source of vitamins (see p. 56).

Promoting health and well-being

Micronutrients

As well as macronutrients, we need **micronutrients** in our diets. These are found in much smaller quantities in foods — sometimes only thousandths of a gram. Micronutrients are either **vitamins** or **minerals**. The vitamins are given letters of the alphabet as names — for example, vitamins A, C and D. Calcium, phosphorus and sodium are common minerals.

Table 4 Vitamins and minerals

Vitamin/mineral	Food sources	What it does
A	Egg yolk, liver, margarine	Helps keep eyes healthy and aids sight in dim light
B (group of vitamins)	Wholegrain cereals, meat, eggs, milk	Helps energy release, normal growth and other cell activities
C	Fresh fruits (especially citrus), tomatoes, peppers, green vegetables, new potatoes	Helps fight infection, heal wounds and maintain gums, ligaments and blood vessels
D	Egg yolk, some fish, margarine; can be made by the action of sunlight on the skin	Helps build strong teeth and bones
K	Dark green leafy vegetables, cheese, pork, liver	Helps blood to clot
Calcium	Milk and dairy products, shellfish, tofu	Helps build bones and teeth, keeps blood clotting and helps muscle and nerve functions
Iron	Red meat, liver, kidneys, plain chocolate, some nuts	Helps make pigment for red blood cells, which carry oxygen around the body
Potassium	Meat, fish, eggs, whole wheat	Helps build teeth and bones
Sodium	Part of salt and therefore added to foods like bacon and cheese; found naturally in fish and other meats	Maintains body fluid balance, helps nerve and muscle function

We need only small amounts of vitamins and minerals to balance our diets, but as you can see they do play important roles in keeping our bodies healthy.

Water

Our bodies are made up of nearly 70% water. Water is part of our cells, blood and other body fluids. It is essential for our cell reactions. We need water to stay alive; without it we would live only for a few days.

Fibre

Fibre is found in wholemeal foods and vegetables. It is needed to help form faeces and for them to pass easily out of the body. Fibre adds bulk to our diet. It is not digested, that is, it is not broken down and used. As it travels through the digestive system, it absorbs water. Fibre is chemically known as non-starch polysaccharides, or NSP for short.

We do not have to worry too much about eating a balanced diet of macronutrients, micronutrients, water and fibre at every meal – provided we balance our diet over a few days or a week. So eating chips every day is not good (too much fat), but once in a while it is OK. With this in mind, we should not think of foods as good or bad. It is our overall diet that matters.

A good balanced diet has a variety of foods in quantities to suit the individual's age, gender and activity level. There are guidelines to help people know how much they should eat. These are sometimes called **dietary reference values**, or DRVs for short. Knowing the DRVs helps individuals to plan a balanced diet.

Many people do not get enough fruit and vegetables in their diets, especially if they eat a lot of ready-made meals or processed foods. A good target is to try to eat five portions of fruit and vegetables every day. A glass of pure fruit juice counts as one portion, but juice can only be one of the five daily portions. Extra fruit juices in the day do not count. 'Five a day' helps supply essential vitamins and fibre and therefore helps to balance the diet.

Fruit and vegetables provide fibre and vitamins in our diet. Try to eat at least five portions each day.

Unit 2: Promoting health and well-being

If you keep a record of food and drink intake, there are a number of ways of analysing your diet. One way is by using computer software. This calculates the amounts of the different macro- and micronutrients and fibre in the diet. Usually, the software provides typical DRVs for individuals of a particular age and gender and compares your diet with these.

Another way is by using food tables. These are books that have tables of data showing the typical quantities of food components in different foods. Analysing the diet in this way takes longer than by computer, but is just as useful.

Most food manufacturers now supply dietary information as part of the labelling and packaging of their food products. This can be a useful source of information when calculating food components eaten.

When calculating and analysing a diet, it is important to take into account relevant details. For example, if you drink a glass of milk, what type of milk is it — whole, semi-skimmed or skimmed — and exactly what quantity of milk is consumed? The more detail recorded, the more accurate the analysis can be.

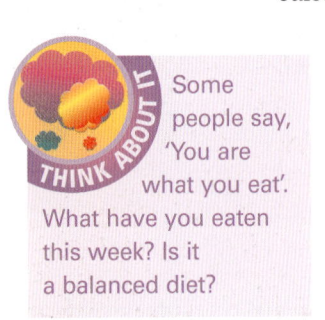

THINK ABOUT IT — Some people say, 'You are what you eat'. What have you eaten this week? Is it a balanced diet?

ACTIVITY — Keep a diet diary and analyse what you eat.

Exercise

Another major factor for keeping healthy is **regular exercise**.

Some people get the exercise they need because of the job they do, while others make exercise part of their leisure activities. Regular exercise is important for individuals of all ages.

It is generally recommended that we exercise for at least 30 minutes five times a week. This means activities like brisk walking, cycling or swimming. For more vigorous activities, such as circuit training or weight lifting, two or three times a week is recommended with at least a day off between sessions. This gives the body time to recover.

There are many physical benefits from regular exercise. Muscles get stronger, the body becomes more toned, better posture develops and a healthy body weight is achieved and maintained. As well as getting stronger, our stamina improves. This means being able to keep physically active for longer — for example, when exercising or just doing everyday physical activities such as carrying shopping or cleaning the house. Another benefit of regular exercise is suppleness. Exercising keeps our joints flexible, making a good range of movement possible. This is useful as we age because our joints become stiffer and lose some mobility.

A long-term benefit of regular exercise is the reduced risk of heart disease. Regular exercise keeps our arteries elastic and prevents plaque

AQA GCSE **Health & Social Care**

building up in them. Plaque forms from cholesterol, a fat-like substance. If the small coronary arteries of the heart become blocked, a heart attack occurs because the heart muscle cells do not receive any blood supply. This cuts off oxygen from the cells. While other factors may help cause this problem, exercise reduces the risk, and even when people do have a heart attack, they are less likely to die if they have exercised regularly.

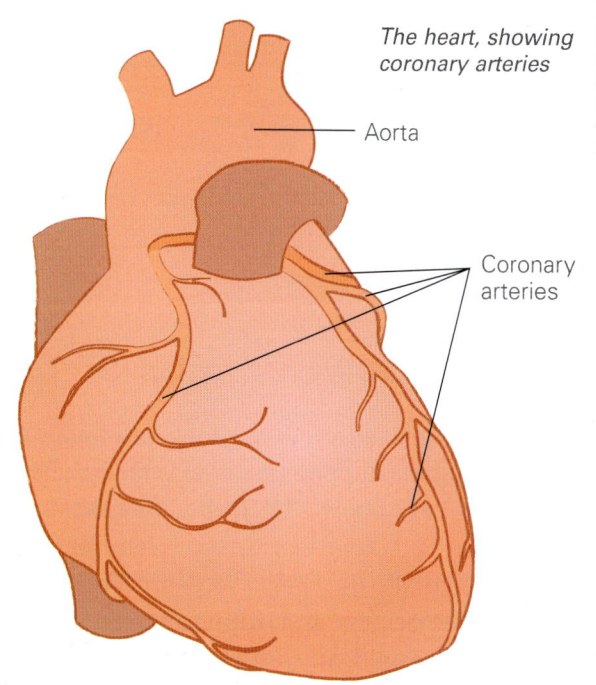

The heart, showing coronary arteries

Aorta

Coronary arteries

Regular exercise is important for people of all ages; some people like to work out in the gym while others enjoy activities such as gardening. Some of us just like to play!

59

Unit 2 Promoting health and well-being

As well as physical benefits, regular exercise can help in other areas of health and well-being. Socially, we might meet new people and make new friends when exercising at the local gym or leisure centre. Emotionally, we will feel good about ourselves. Intellectually we can concentrate better as exercise clears the mind and helps us think problems through.

ACTIVITY

Create an exercise diary for yourself for the next week. Record the types and times you exercise. How much do you do?

Exercise diary

	Date	Activity	Time
e.g.	5.3.07	Walked to school	20 mins

Supportive relationships

From when we are very young, our family and particularly our parents provide many different forms of support. Physically, they make sure we are fed, kept warm, kept clean and safe. Intellectually, they help us to learn. Emotionally, we feel secure and supported and able to develop confidently as individuals. Socially, we interact with our family and learn to develop the social skills necessary when meeting others and making friends.

As we get older, our relationships change. Parents may lose influence over us while friends become more important. Although we become independent individuals, we still need support from those closest to us.

We also form relationships with other people who we meet in our everyday lives. While not as close as family or friends, these relationships are important. Teachers and other school staff,

GPs and other health workers and, later in life, people we meet through work all play a part in helping us to develop and maintain our health and well-being.

Adequate financial resources

Having enough money is an important positive factor affecting health and well-being. We need money for **essentials**. These are the items we need to stay alive. We also need money for **non-essentials**. These are the items we want but do not need. If we have enough money, we are able to pay for all the essentials such as food and clothes, and have some money over for non-essentials such as DVDs and mobile phones. Meeting needs and wants helps support the different aspects of our health and well-being.

> **ACTIVITY**
> Choose a television soap and draw a relationship map (a 'bubble' diagram) for all the characters. Use thick lines between the characters for close relationships and thin ones for other relationships.

> **THINK ABOUT IT**
> How does having enough money affect a person physically, emotionally and socially?

> **ACTIVITY**
> Draw up a 'wants and needs' table for yourself.

Stimulating work, education and leisure activity

No one likes being bored or being in a job they hate. Doing well at school and getting good results in exams helps people to feel good about themselves. This helps their emotional health and well-being. It also helps when starting work. Individuals with good qualifications have a better choice of job or career than other people with fewer qualifications. The person with good qualifications is also more likely to succeed in the selection process for a particular job. Finding work that is interesting and challenging mentally develops our knowledge, understanding and problem-solving abilities. By keeping our minds active we develop mental skills and so help our intellectual health and well-being.

Unit 2 Promoting health and well-being

Using leisure time well also helps. Everybody needs time to relax but that does not mean not using our brains. A lot of leisure activities exercise the mind while helping people to rest. Crosswords and quizzes like Sudoku are good examples.

Reading is another activity that helps stimulate the imagination. We learn new words and phrases, while increasing our vocabulary and understanding. Hobbies such as playing a musical instrument also help stimulate the mind. As we get older, exercising the mind is believed to help prevent dementia, so it is a good idea to 'use it, not lose it' when it comes to our brain power.

Keeping the balance between work and leisure helps reduce an individual's stress levels. All work and no play is not a good idea as both our bodies and our minds need time to rest and recover to stay healthy and well.

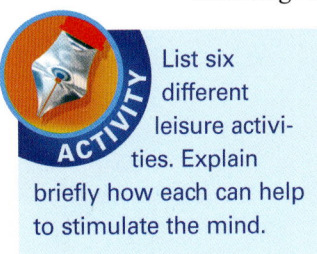

ACTIVITY
List six different leisure activities. Explain briefly how each can help to stimulate the mind.

Health monitoring and illness prevention services

Health monitoring begins even before we are born. As babies develop in the womb, their growth and development are monitored to check progress. For example, ultrasound images are taken of the fetus.

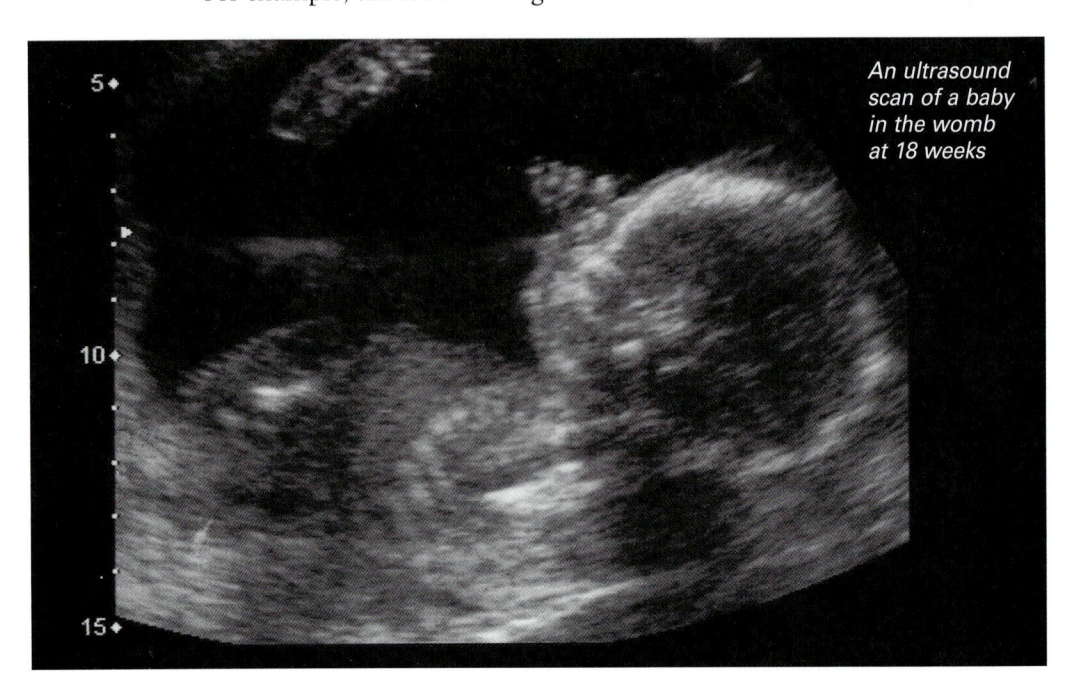

An ultrasound scan of a baby in the womb at 18 weeks

Immunisation

Babies and young children are immunised to prevent infectious diseases such as diphtheria, polio, tetanus, whooping cough (pertussis), measles, mumps and rubella (German measles). These immunisations are vitally important because it takes time for an individual's immunity to develop. Immunity is built up by giving weakened versions of the disease. To build up immunisation successfully, a series of injections/vaccinations is given over time. A typical immunisation programme is shown in Table 5.

Age	Immunisation	How
2 months	Diphtheria Tetanus Pertussis (whooping cough) Polio Hib (influenza)	One injection
	Pneumonia	One injection
3 months	Diphtheria Tetanus Pertussis (whooping cough) Polio Hib (influenza)	One injection
	Meningitis	One injection
4 months	Diphtheria Tetanus Pertussis (whooping cough) Polio Hib (influenza)	One injection
	Meningitis	One injection
	Pneumonia	One injection
12 months	Meningitis and Hib	One injection
13 months	MMR (measles, mumps, rubella)	One injection
	Pneumonia	One injection
3–5 years	Diphtheria Tetanus Pertussis (whooping cough) Polio	One injection
	MMR	One injection
13–18 years	Diphtheria Tetanus Polio	One injection

Table 5 Immunisation programme

Unit 2

Promoting health and well-being

Screening tests

Different screening tests are carried out to detect risk factors linked with disease or to diagnose illness so that early treatment can be given. Some common screening tests for adults are blood pressure measurements, blood cholesterol tests, cervical smears and mammograms for breast cancer.

Blood cholesterol tests

When measuring blood cholesterol, individuals are asked not to have anything to eat for 12 hours before the test (except water, tea or coffee without milk). A blood sample is taken and the cholesterol content measured. There is a close link between high blood cholesterol levels and heart disease. Individuals with high levels of blood cholesterol can then be treated to reduce the risk.

Cervical smear tests

This test is carried out to help doctors find women who may be likely to develop cancer in the neck of the womb (the cervix). This cancer is one of the most common cancers to affect women. The doctor or nurse takes a sample by gently scraping some of cells from the neck of the womb. Ideally this is done halfway between one period and the next. The cells are

Light micrograph of a cervical smear, showing abnormal cells at the top and normal cells at the bottom

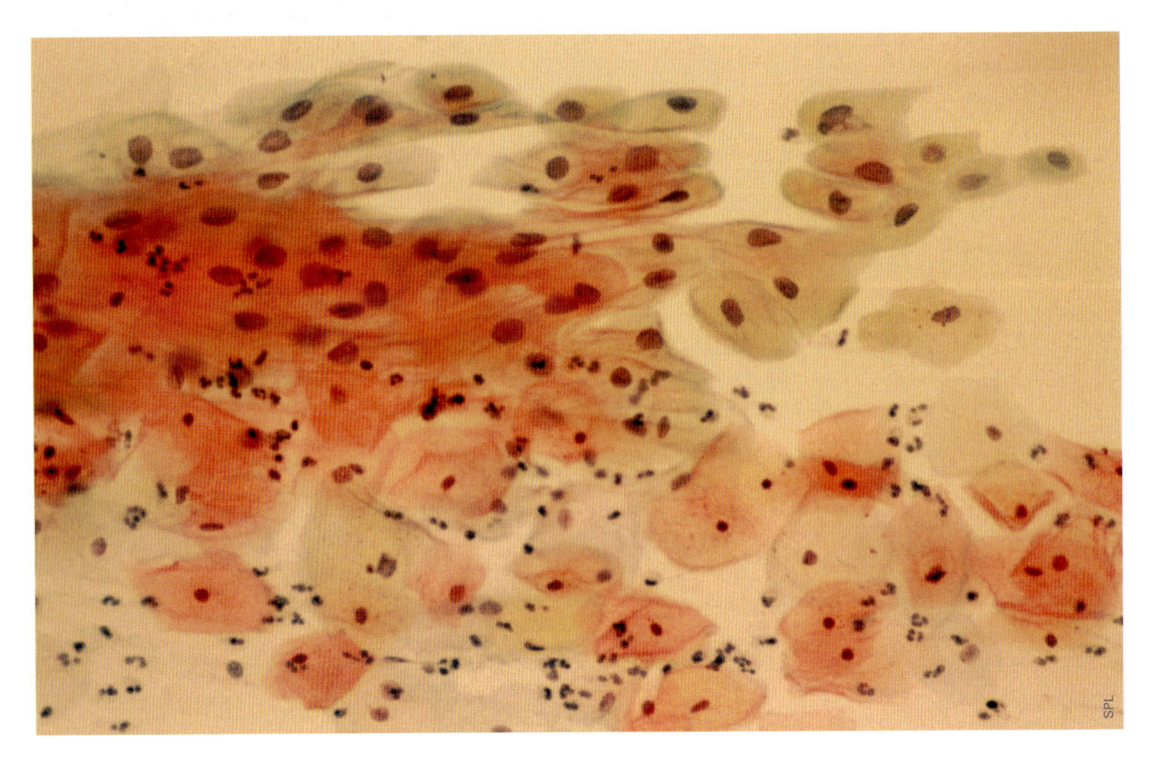

smeared onto a glass slide and can then be examined under a microscope. If cancer is likely to develop, some abnormal cells will be seen. In these cases, preventative treatment can be given to the woman.

Women between the ages of 25 and 65 are invited for regular cervical smear tests. Between 25 and 49 years of age, the test is done every 3 years; from 50 to 64 it is done every 5 years. After the age of 65, only those with recent abnormal tests are offered another test.

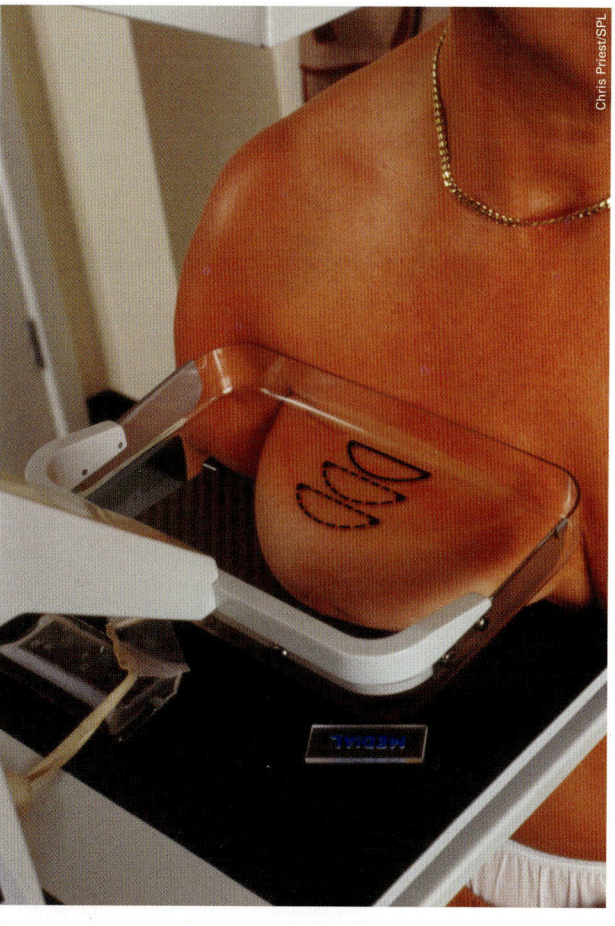

Mammograms

Women aged 50 and up to the age of 70 are invited for breast cancer screening every 3 years. This means around 1.5 million women are screened every year. In mammography, an image is taken by flattening each breast in turn and sending a pulse of X-rays through it. The image is examined for abnormal cells that may be cancerous. Not all abnormalities are dangerous cancers. Further investigation is needed if abnormalities are found. It is estimated that out of every 10 000 women screened, about 500 will be recalled for further assessment. Of these, about 80 will need an operation and 60 out of the 80 will have cancer.

A woman undergoing a mammogram

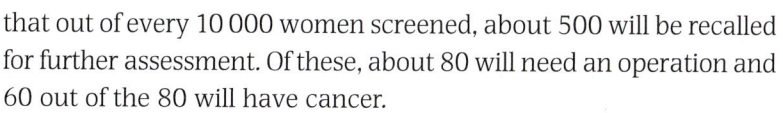

When screening tests show something is wrong, treatment can be given to protect our physical health. When the tests show nothing is wrong, it gives us peace of mind knowing all is well. This helps our emotional well-being by reducing anxiety.

ACTIVITY: Find out how blood pressure tests are performed and why they are important.

Risk management

All activities in life carry some degree of risk. Some activities are considered high risk because there is a good chance that an accident may occur and physical damage — perhaps severe, as in horse-riding accidents — may

Unit 2

Promoting health and well-being

result. Even everyday activities such as crossing the road have some risk attached. While not all risks can be removed completely, we can reduce them considerably. In the case of horse-riding, it is much safer if the correct equipment is used and participants are fully trained. When crossing the road, we should always check for oncoming traffic.

Under the **Health and Safety at Work Act**, everybody in a workplace has a responsibility to keep themselves and others safe from harm. Being able to recognise risks to health and well-being is important if accidents are to be avoided. Carrying out a formal risk assessment is recommended. Reducing the likelihood of accidents by acting carefully and responsibly is called risk management.

Snow boarding is a high-risk activity

ACTIVITY
Carry out a risk assessment in your home or at school. Identify possible risks to health and well-being. Suggest one way in which each risk could be reduced or eliminated.

Many risks to our physical health and well-being may be fairly obvious, but others may not be so evident. People who are bullied, abused or left out of group activities are at risk emotionally and socially. In these cases, individuals can lose confidence and self-esteem and become isolated and withdrawn. Young children and the elderly are often particularly vulnerable in these circumstances if they rely on other people to care for them.

Factors causing risks to health and well-being

There are many **lifestyle factors** that can cause risks to health and well-being. Some of these can be controlled — for example, substance misuse or lack of regular physical exercise. However, some factors cannot be changed — for example, the genetic make-up we inherit.

Genetically inherited diseases and conditions

When a sperm fertilises an egg, it brings together the genetic information needed to create life. The combination of genes in the fertilised egg determines many aspects of how the individual develops — for example, his/her eye colour and blood group type. Sometimes the inheritance of one or more defective genes causes a disorder, which affects different aspects of health and well-being.

Some examples of inherited disorders caused by defective genes are shown in Table 6. These defective genes all cause physical effects in the individual, which may, in turn, affect other aspects of health and well-being.

THINK ABOUT IT
How might red–green colour blindness affect a person's health and well-being?

Inherited disorder	Effects
Albinism	Lack of pigment (melanin) so the person's skin, hair and eyes are not coloured
Phenylketonuria	Causes an enzyme deficiency, so some proteins in the person's diet are not digested; can cause brain damage if not treated
Colour blindness	Reduced ability to tell certain colours apart (e.g. red–green); affects more males than females
Haemophilia	Causes a person's blood not to clot or to clot slowly; affects more males than females
Huntington's disease	A brain disorder that develops in adulthood and causes abnormal movements and progressive dementia

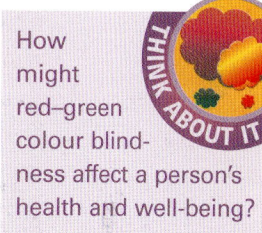

Table 6
Inherited disorders

Substance misuse

Medical drugs are chemical substances that help treat the causes and symptoms of different diseases and disorders. Recreational drugs, such as

Unit 2

Promoting health and well-being

alcohol and tobacco, are used to change a person's moods and feelings. These examples of drugs are legal. Some illegal drugs are also used as recreational drugs — for example, heroin and cannabis.

Virtually all drugs are addictive and carry the risk that the user's health and the health and well-being of those around them can be seriously affected.

Using medical drugs for purposes other than they were intended is dangerous misuse. For example, the sleeping drug temazepam is sometimes used as a recreational drug. When people are addicted to a drug, they crave more of it. This means they have a physical, emotional and/or psychological dependence on the drug. Addicted drug users are likely to try to increase the amount of drug they take, because the effect gets less as time goes on. If they are unable to get the drug, they suffer from unpleasant physical reactions called withdrawal symptoms. These can include vomiting or nausea, shaking, sweating, confusion, irritability and agitation. Drug addicts usually need specialist help and treatment to lose their addiction.

Being addicted to drugs can be expensive. Individuals may find themselves spending more and more money to satisfy their cravings. This can affect other aspects of their lives — for example, they have less money for food, clothing and bills. Many addicts are tempted into crime as a way of funding their addictions.

Drinking more than the recommended number of units of alcohol each week can seriously damage your health

Alcohol

Drinking alcohol in moderation is safe and enjoyable. Some evidence suggests that small amounts of alcohol, for example a glass of red wine each day, can help to prevent heart disease and strokes. However, more alcohol can actually damage the heart muscle. Drinking more than the recommended number of units of alcohol each week can cause other serious problems. The current recommendations are:

+ 14 units per week for women
+ 21 units per week for men

Some sources recommend no more than:

+ 21 units per week for women
+ 28 units per week for men

Alcopops usually contain 1.5 units of alcohol; a glass of wine contains 1–1.5 units; spirits such as whisky, gin and vodka have 1 unit per standard measure; beers and lagers contain 1–2 units per half pint; strong beers and lagers have more units, depending on their strength.

The gender difference for units of alcohol per week is mainly to do with the different body composition of adult males and females and the fact that males are generally bigger. Another view on drinking is that people should not drink every day, even within the weekly limits. Alcohol-free days are recommended to give the body, especially the liver, time to recover.

'Binge' drinking of more than 4–5 units of alcohol a day is becoming a major problem. When people are drunk, it often leads to violence and disorder, and an increased likelihood of having an accident or being the victim of crime.

Major physical health problems associated with alcohol misuse are:

+ *Liver disease* This starts as fatty liver where fat builds up in liver cells. This can develop into hepatitis, when the liver becomes inflamed. Eventually, if heavy drinking of alcohol continues, liver cirrhosis may occur. Normal liver tissue is replaced by scar tissue. This can lead to liver failure.
+ *Brain cell damage* Alcohol is a depressant drug and it can affect the brain, as heavy drinkers find. When drinking, they may have blurred vision, slurred speech, slowed reaction times, impaired memory and difficulty walking. Regular heavy drinking can cause long-term problems by damaging brain cells, resulting in the person becoming confused and disoriented.
+ *Damaging the fetus in pregnancy* It is dangerous for females to drink large quantities of alcohol during pregnancy, as this can cause physical and mental problems for the baby. Birth defects due to drinking alcohol during pregnancy include babies with learning disabilities, hyperactivity, short attention span, sleeping problems and behavioural difficulties. Most of these problems can last throughout life.

Alcohol can be enjoyed at social events but should be consumed in limited quantities

Unit 2: Promoting health and well-being

- *High blood pressure* Regular alcohol consumption can lead to high blood pressure, which is called hypertension. It is believed to be the third largest cause of high blood pressure in adults. Exactly how alcohol causes this problem is not understood. It is believed that the major cause is the effect of alcohol on the liver and hormone activity.
- *Strokes* Strokes caused by blood clots are more common in heavy drinkers than in other groups. This is linked to high blood pressure, especially where arteries narrow and blood flow to the brain is slowed.

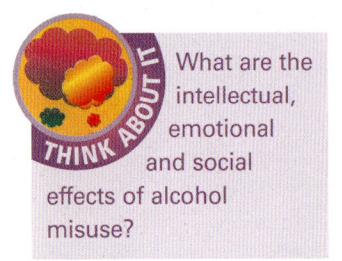

Many people, including doctors, are concerned about the increasing problems of underage drinking. Heavy drinking by young people carries greater risks as their bodies are still developing. They are also likely to become addicted to alcohol and form a pattern of alcohol abuse in later life.

Organisations such as Alcoholics Anonymous help people with alcohol-related problems.

> **THINK ABOUT IT** What are the intellectual, emotional and social effects of alcohol misuse?

Smoking

Smoking is highly addictive due to the nicotine in the tobacco. Nicotine is a mild stimulant, and it affects the brain quickly. When smoke is inhaled, nicotine affects the brain within 8 seconds. It also raises the smoker's blood pressure. The smoke releases many other harmful substances, including tar and carbon monoxide. Tar irritates and inflames the lungs. Carbon monoxide prevents the blood carrying as much oxygen as it should. Breathing in the smoke from the air is called passive smoking. Smoke from burning cigarettes, cigars and pipes and also exhaled by smokers is called environmental tobacco smoke (ETS). This can cause the same health problems in non-smokers that smokers are prone to. For this reason, no-smoking policies are being extended to more and more public places. There is no safe use of tobacco.

The risks to health and well-being associated with smoking are:

- lung cancer and cancers of the mouth and throat; lung cancer kills more people than any other form of cancer
- coronary heart disease due to raised blood pressure and blocked arteries; smokers in their 30s and 40s are five times more likely to have a heart attack than non-smokers of the same age
- circulatory problems, such as deep vein thrombosis, which can lead to limb amputations
- strokes; about one-quarter of these are linked to smoking

- lowered fetal birth weight and greater risk of death of the baby just after birth if the pregnant mother smokes
- premature ageing of the skin; it is estimated that the skin of a 40-year-old smoker is often as wrinkled as that of a 60-year-old non-smoker
- early menopause; smokers generally experience menopause 2 years before non-smokers
- lowered male fertility; smoking reduces numbers of healthy sperm; studies show that smoking also increases the risk of men becoming impotent, that is, unable to maintain an erection

Illegal drugs

There are many different types of illegal drug. Common ones are:

- cannabis
- cocaine
- heroin
- ecstasy
- LSD
- magic mushrooms

Cannabis is considered a 'soft' drug, as opposed to 'hard' drugs such as cocaine and heroin. Cannabis contains more than 400 chemicals, some of which can cause cancer. In fact, there is a greater concentration of these in cannabis than in tobacco. All soft drugs are still illegal. Cannabis decreases coordination and concentration and may cause anxiety and paranoia when taken. Long-term damage includes respiratory disorders, memory problems and mental illness, together with general apathy.

Cocaine is a 'hard' drug that acts as a stimulant. Cocaine addiction leads to lethargy and depression, paranoia and possibly heart attacks. Sniffing the drug causes damage to nose and lung tissues. Crack is cocaine that has been processed so that it can be smoked. While cocaine or crack makes the user feel 'high', this is followed by a 'crash' during which the person feels anxious and irritable.

Heroin is a 'hard' drug extracted from the opium poppy. It is a fast-acting drug giving instant feelings of well-being. It can cause anxiety and fear,

Unit 2: Promoting health and well-being

blurred vision, constricted pupils, slow breathing, nausea and vomiting. Heroin is highly addictive and large doses can cause coma and even death. If heroin is injected using a shared needle, there is a risk of contracting human immunodeficiency virus (HIV). The virus attacks the immune system and can cause coma, blood vessel damage, tremors and apathy. The person may develop AIDS.

Pure ecstasy is a white powder usually sold as a tablet. Its effects develop after about 30 minutes, giving the user an energy 'buzz'. The down side is that the body can overheat and dehydrate, which can lead to death. Over 200 people have died from this drug in recent years. Its use is linked to liver, kidney and heart problems, as well as paranoia and depression.

LSD is lysergic acid diethylamide, which is a hallucinogenic drug. This means it causes users to have delusions (mistaken ideas) about what is happening around them. They will see things, hear sounds and feel sensations that seem real but do not exist. Sometimes these feel good, sometimes quite the opposite. People have been known to jump from windows or in front of cars while under the influence of LSD. LSD can

Anti-drugs campaigns encourage the public to report drug dealers

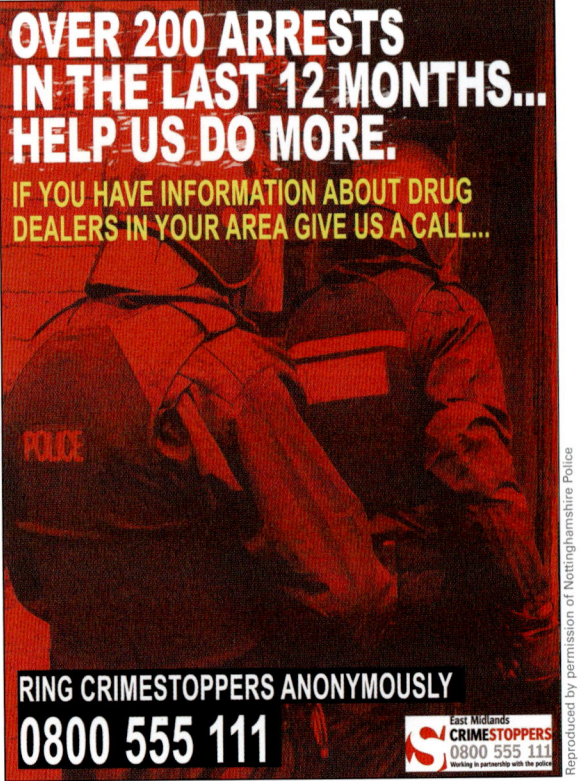

cause long-lasting damage, including **schizophrenia** and severe depression.

Magic mushrooms have similar effects to LSD, as they are hallucinogenic. However, they also increase heart rate and blood pressure and can cause severe stomach pains, diarrhoea and sickness. There is the added danger that magic mushrooms can be confused with other poisonous fungi.

Once addicted to any drug, it is difficult to control the amount being taken, and overdoses are common. Overdosing on 'hard' drugs often causes death.

Drugs and the law

Illegal drugs are classified into three groups: A, B and C. Each class has a set of possible fines and jail sentences that can be given for possession or supply of the drugs. Being convicted of a drugs-related offence can have a serious impact on a person's health and well-being.

> **Definition**
> **Schizophrenia** is a mental disorder where sufferers have delusions and hallucinations and may behave in a bizarre manner or without purpose.

> **Activity**
> Research one illegal drug in detail. Produce a wall display or give a presentation on the dangers to health and well-being it causes.

Class	Examples	Maximum sentence for Possession	Supply
A	Crack cocaine, cocaine, ecstasy, heroin, LSD, magic mushrooms (prepared for use), methadone; any class B drug prepared for injection	7 years in prison and/or unlimited fine	Life in prison and/or unlimited fine
B	Amphetamines, codeine in concentrations above 2.5%, Ritalin, barbiturates	5 years in prison and/or unlimited fine	14 years in prison and/or unlimited fine
C	Cannabis*, anabolic steroids, tranquillisers including Valium and Rohypnol	2 years in prison and/or unlimited fine	5 years in prison and/or unlimited fine

Table 7
Drug classes

*Cannabis was reclassified as a class C drug in January 2004.

Solvents

Solvents are not illegal drugs, but their sale to those under 18 *is* illegal. They are found in glue, petrol and aerosols, and are addictive if inhaled. They cause a dream-like state but they can cause vomiting and loss of consciousness, and possibly even death. In the long term, the user develops a cough and a rash around the nose and mouth. The brain, nervous system, liver and kidneys can be damaged.

Unit 2 Promoting health and well-being

Unbalanced, poor-quality or inadequate diet

In the UK today there are more overweight and obese people than ever before. The main cause of this is overeating. Taking in more food than we need means that the surplus is stored as fat somewhere in the body. This causes a strain on heart muscle and blood circulation, and increases the risk of heart disease, high blood pressure, type 2 diabetes, hernias and varicose veins. Self-confidence and esteem are often low in obese people.

Eating too little food is less common, but also causes problems. People who eat too little become underweight, lack energy and are prone to infections. Repair and maintenance of body tissues may suffer.

Some individuals suffer from eating disorders. Anyone can be affected, but the most likely sufferers are young women between the ages of 15 and 25. The three most common eating disorders are anorexia nervosa, bulimia and compulsive/binge eating.

Anorexia nervosa

People suffering from anorexia nervosa strive to achieve a very low 'ideal' weight. This may involve avoiding food, taking excessive exercise, using laxatives or diuretics and/or inducing vomiting. The weight loss can have severe physical effects on the body – for example, stopping periods and causing other hormonal problems.

Bulimia

There are different forms of this disorder. The person 'binges', that is, eats large quantities of food (often carbohydrates) in a short time. To prevent weight gain, the person then restricts his/her food intake, forces vomiting, abuses laxatives and/or exercises excessively. After vomiting, the cycle may be repeated.

Binge eating

This is similar to bulimia. The individual loses control over his/her eating and consumes large amounts of food even when not hungry. This is accompanied by feelings of guilt or disgust at having eaten so much. Unlike bulimia sufferers, however, binge eaters do not try to get rid of the food eaten.

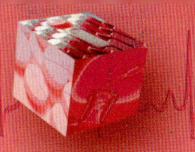

Diet balance

Apart from eating the correct amount of food, it is important to have, broadly, the correct balance of food components in the diet. An imbalanced diet can lead to health problems. For example, too much salt can cause high blood pressure, while too little fibre can cause constipation and other intestinal disorders. Vitamin and mineral deficiency disorders are extremely rare in the developed world and there is little evidence that eating too many of these micronutrients causes problems.

When trying to plan a balanced diet it is important to consider:

+ the cost of foods
+ how they are to be prepared (for example, grilling or frying can make a big difference)
+ the personal food preferences of the individual
+ the availability of the chosen foods

The labelling of food products makes the food component information more readily available. This helps people to make informed choices about the foods they eat.

Obesity leads to many different kinds of health problems and is causing increasing concern among doctors

Calories	Fat	Saturates	Sugars	Salt
350	11.2g	4.8g	4.8g	2.3g

approx. per pack

Oven cook in 40 mins | Microwave in 8½ mins | Suitable for freezing | Serves 1 400g ℮

Nutrition

Typical Values	per 100g	per pack		GDA Average adult
Energy Value	370 kJ	1480 kJ		
(Calories	90 kcal	350 kcal)		2000 kcal
Protein	5.1 g	20.4 g		45 g
Carbohydrate	10.6 g	42.4 g		230 g
(of which Sugars	1.2 g	4.8 g)	Low	90 g
Fat	2.8 g	11.2 g	Low	70 g
(of which Saturates	1.2 g	4.8 g)	Low	20 g
Fibre	1.3 g	5.2 g		24 g
Sodium	0.2 g	0.9 g		2.4 g
Salt	0.6 g	2.3 g	Med	6 g

GDA = Guideline Daily Amounts

Serving suggestion

Food labelling can help us to make healthier choices about our diet

Unit 2 Promoting health and well-being

> **ACTIVITY**
>
> Analyse Tim's typical daily diet for 'balance'. Use dietary software or food tables, if available, to help.
>
> Tim's typical daily diet
>
> | | |
> |---|---|
> | Breakfast: | 2 slices of toast made from white bread
butter and marmalade
tea with whole milk and 2 teaspoons of sugar |
> | Snack: | 1 bag of crisps (standard size)
1 can of non-diet cola |
> | Lunch: | 1 portion of chips and gravy |
> | Tea: | 1 baked potato and butter
1 green salad containing lettuce, cucumber and spring onions |
> | Snack: | 1 chocolate bar
1 coffee with whole milk and 2 sugars |
>
> What would you recommend to help Tim improve his diet?

Too much stress

Stress is the term given to the physical and intellectual demands put on the body. It is not automatically a bad thing. We sometimes perform better when slightly stressed — for example, during examinations. Sometimes stress is short term, such as narrowly avoiding an accident when driving a car. At other times, stress is more long term, such as ongoing pressures in a relationship. Short-term stress is sometimes called acute stress. It demands a lot of energy and can make the person feel drained. Long-term stress is sometimes called chronic stress. The body reacts to this type of stress slowly. Individuals can become used to living with a certain level of tension. This form of stress can be ignored until the body shows signs of it.

Some life events, for example divorce and **redundancy**, are potentially stressful. Not all events carry the same degree of stress — a divorce is highly stressful compared with going on a diet.

Individuals react differently to the same situation or event, so the amount of stress experienced varies.

Stress causes physical reactions in the body. Heart rate increases and sweating occurs. With ongoing stress, the person may suffer tension headaches, muscle pains and general feelings of tiredness.

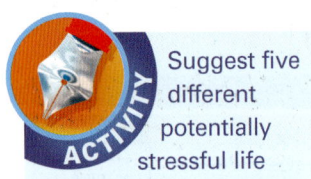

> **ACTIVITY**
>
> Suggest five different potentially stressful life events. Explain how each one can cause raised stress levels.

> **Definition**
>
> **Redundancy** is the loss of a job through being no longer needed by the employer.

In more extreme cases, high blood pressure, irritable bowel syndrome and mental disorders can occur.

A person under stress may feel anxious, irritable or tearful. Decision-making becomes difficult, sleep patterns are disturbed and appetite may be lost. Under these circumstances, people may turn to drugs such as alcohol or tobacco. These are not effective as long-term solutions.

It is important to identify the cause of the stress and work to minimise its effects. Support from friends and family, taking part in non-stressful exercise and leisure activities, and relaxation exercises and techniques can all help. What is most important is not to ignore increased stress. Professional help is available for individuals who have difficulty managing stress. This can be accessed through the local GP.

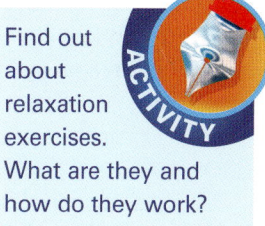

ACTIVITY

Find out about relaxation exercises. What are they and how do they work?

Yoga is great exercise for flexibility, strength and relaxation

Lack of personal hygiene

It is important to wash regularly, at least once a day, using soap and water, to maintain personal hygiene. This removes sweat, dead skin cells and oily secretions from the body surface. Microorganisms such as bacteria build up their numbers by using these bodily substances as food sources. Daily washing prevents microorganisms from multiplying.

Unit 2 Promoting health and well-being

ACTIVITY

Washing regularly is just one way to maintain personal hygiene. Make a list of ten other ways. Here are two to start you off: keeping fingernails short, changing underwear daily.

It is especially important to wash your hands after handling dirty objects, going to the toilet and before handling food. Microorganisms are easily transferred from one person to another via food, personal physical contact or handling objects touched by the other person. Young children need help to maintain their personal hygiene as they are not able to manage it themselves. Some older people may also need help as they become frail.

Failure to wash regularly and maintain good personal hygiene results in **body odour**, or BO for short. The smell is created by the activity of microorganisms on the skin. Having a bad body odour is not just unpleasant but also causes embarrassment and discomfort.

Bad breath, which is called halitosis, is a problem that may be caused by poor oral hygiene. Regular brushing and flossing the teeth and gums, together with regular dental check-ups, can help to solve the problem. Some individuals find that they need to use a tongue scraper and/or breath mints and mouthwashes. Drinking plenty of water also helps. Even friends will not want to be near an individual who smells, so social health and well-being is affected. In time, this can affect the individual emotionally as they may lose confidence and self-esteem.

Other problems associated with poor hygiene include infestation from parasites such as threadworms, ringworm (a fungus) and scabies (a mite). A fungus that thrives in the sweaty conditions found between the toes causes athlete's foot. Washing and drying your feet well is important to prevent athlete's foot developing. Impetigo is a skin infection that spreads easily under conditions of poor personal hygiene. Impetigo first appears as

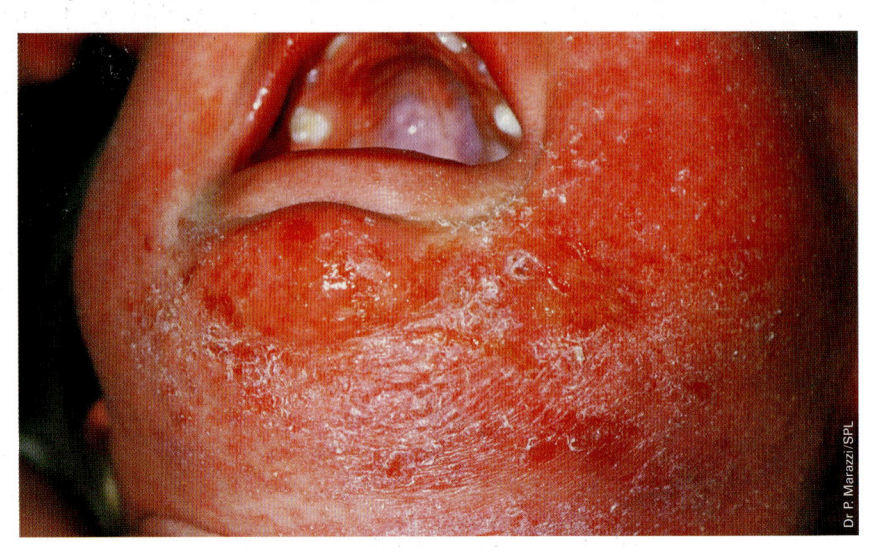

Impetigo rash around a baby's chin

a small scratch or itchy patch of skin. This small, red, itchy spot soon develops into a blister containing a yellow substance. Later, the top of the blister becomes crusty and fluid leaks out. New blisters form in the same region or on other parts of the body, usually the face, around the mouth, nose and back of the ears. Impetigo spreads quickly through contact, but can be treated by washing with soap and water and letting the affected areas dry in the air. GPs may prescribe ointments to help.

ACTIVITY Find out about the causes and effects of:
+ threadworms
+ ringworm
+ scabies

Lack of regular exercise

Lack of regular exercise is linked to many health and well-being problems. These include increased risks of:
+ coronary heart disease
+ heart attacks (and less chance of surviving them)
+ weight gain and obesity
+ raised blood cholesterol
+ high blood pressure
+ loss of mobility and flexibility
+ reduced strength and stamina
+ back pain

Coronary heart disease and heart attacks are often linked to raised blood cholesterol and high blood pressure. When the coronary arteries delivering blood to the heart muscle become blocked, a heart attack can occur. The heart muscle has no supply of oxygen and cannot remove carbon dioxide and other waste materials. The heart stops pumping blood efficiently or may stop altogether. In England, around 275 000 people suffer a heart attack every year. Coronary heart disease kills more than 110 000 people, making it the biggest killer in the country.

Weight gain can lead to obesity, which reduces a person's mobility and flexibility. Extra pressure is put onto the person's joints. Without regular exercise, the individual's muscles are not maintained. They lose the ability to act powerfully, so the person loses strength. In addition, the person's ability to keep going, that is, his/her endurance or stamina, is reduced. This means the person's ability to do everyday tasks such as cleaning and carrying shopping decreases.

Weight gain and loss of muscle strength often cause back pain as pressure is put on the discs in the spine. Exercising regularly strengthens the muscles and helps hold the discs apart.

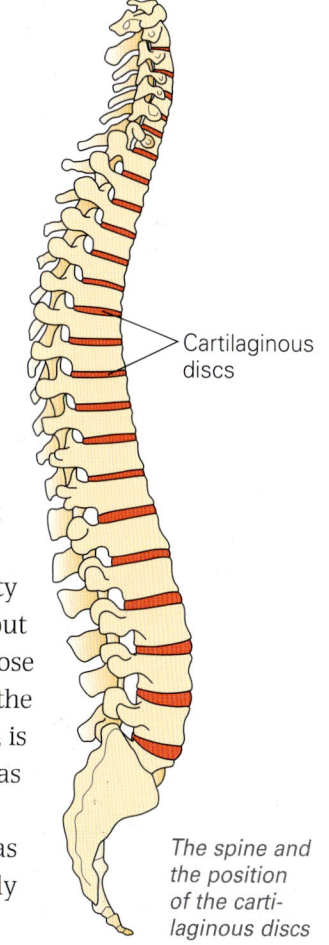

Cartilaginous discs

The spine and the position of the cartilaginous discs

Unit 2 Promoting health and well-being

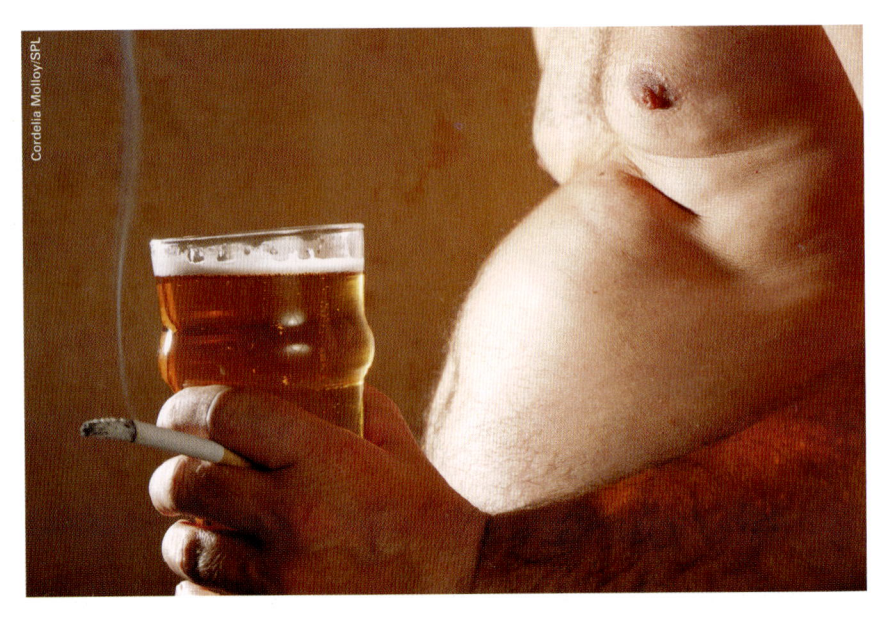

All of these risks are increased considerably if the person is a smoker, drinks alcohol in excess and/or eats a poor, unbalanced diet.

Individuals who do not exercise regularly also miss out on the opportunity to meet new people and make new friends at gyms and sports clubs.

Unprotected sex

Condoms are a barrier method of contraception; they help to prevent unwanted pregnancies as well as sexually transmitted diseases

Unprotected sex is sexual intercourse without the use of a condom or similar barrier. In male–female relationships, pregnancy can occur unless some form of contraception is used. One of the main risks of unprotected sex is therefore unwanted pregnancy.

Unprotected sex allows an exchange of bodily fluids between the partners, which can cause health problems. These problems are mainly **sexually transmitted infections** (STIs). Where a couple remain faithful to each other and have no other sexual partners, no risk is involved.

The most common STI in the UK today is called chlamydial pelvic infection. It is caused by a bacterium that infects the cervix (neck of the womb) in women. Men can carry the infection. There are often no symptoms in women but the bacterium can inflame the male urethra (the tube from the bladder through the penis), causing discomfort.

Other STIs are gonorrhoea, syphilis, trichonomoniasis, genital herpes and genital warts. Human immunodeficiency virus (HIV), which can lead to acquired immunodeficiency syndrome (AIDS), can also be transferred during unprotected sex.

Pelvic infections from unprotected sex can cause female infertility. In addition, having unprotected sex at a young age appears to increase a woman's risk of suffering from cervical cancer late in life.

> **ACTIVITY**
>
> Produce a wall display on one STI other than chlamydia. Include the cause, effects and any statistical evidence you can find about how many people in the UK suffer from it.

Social isolation

People generally choose to be on their own for some periods of time but not all the time. Interactions with other people help develop our relationships and emotional well-being. If we do not have these interactions, we are said to be socially isolated. Choosing to live alone, however, does not mean that a person is socially isolated. There may be many interactions with people at work, and with friends and family. Being isolated socially does not automatically mean that there are no other people around us to interact with. Individuals are just as much at risk of being socially isolated living in the middle of a busy city as they are living on their own, miles from anybody else.

Social isolation can affect people who live in a busy city

Unit 2

Promoting health and well-being

When people are socially isolated, they may feel lonely and sad and can become depressed. Self-esteem can be reduced as a feeling of worthlessness develops. Elderly people may experience social isolation as they lose contact with work colleagues when they retire and they and their friends may find it difficult to get out and about due to failing health. Elderly people in these situations are vulnerable and often at risk physically. If an elderly person is socially isolated and falls ill, or has an accident such as a fall, there may be no one available to help. For this reason, elderly people living on their own are encouraged to have alarm buttons and contact telephone numbers for professional carers. Social services monitor many vulnerable elderly clients and help organise regular homecare assistance.

Poverty

Poverty is a lack of material resources, essentially due to lack of money. People who do not have enough money to meet their basic needs are at high risk of ill health. Generally, people in such a position are either homeless or living in depressed, run-down areas in poor housing conditions. They may have difficulty keeping warm. Their diet might be inadequate in terms of both amount of food available and the balance

ACTIVITY

Poverty affects different aspects of health and well-being. Complete a table like the one below to show the intellectual, emotional and social health and well-being effects of poverty.

The effects of poverty

Intellectual effects	Emotional effects	Social effects

of food components. Foods high in fats and carbohydrates are generally cheap and are likely to provide a high proportion of the diet. All of these factors can seriously damage a person's physical health.

Children born into poverty are more likely to have poor health than those born to more affluent parents. Infant mortality is higher and birth weights are generally lower for families with less money.

Inadequate housing

Everyone needs somewhere to live. A house, bungalow or flat can be bought or rented.

We need a place to provide physical shelter and to be able to relax in safety and security. However, not all housing is of an appropriate standard. It may be considered inadequate if it:

+ is in a poor state of repair
+ lacks basic amenities (e.g. shower or bath facilities)
+ is overcrowded
+ is poorly heated or ventilated

Which of these types of housing do you think might be considered inadequate?

Unit 2 Promoting health and well-being

About half of all serious accidents take place in the home and poor housing conditions may contribute to some of these. For example, falls can result from poor lighting or insecure floor coverings. Carbon monoxide poisoning can occur where old or malfunctioning gas appliances and heating systems are used.

Housing that is in a poor state of repair may be difficult to keep clean and warm. Damp, mould and condensation all contribute to illnesses. House dust mites and pet fur may trigger asthma attacks and allergies in susceptible individuals. Without basic amenities, personal hygiene may suffer. When living in overcrowded conditions, stress levels rise and individuals are more at risk of catching and passing on infectious diseases.

This infection risk is even greater with poor ventilation. Overcrowding is also linked to certain mental health problems. In addition, children in stressful home environments may suffer sleeping problems. Where heating is poor, the very young and the elderly are especially at risk as they have more difficulty in maintaining body temperature. In extreme cases, hypothermia can occur. This is when body temperature falls below 35°C (it is normally 37°C). At this dangerously lower temperature, individuals can become unconscious and might die.

> **ACTIVITY**
> Research the main changes in housing conditions over the past 100–150 years. Your local library and/or museum may be able to help. Find out how basic amenities provision has changed.

Unemployment

Being out of work is a stressful experience. People are naturally anxious about their future when they are not earning a living. While the national benefits system supports individuals during unemployment, this only provides financial support at a basic level. As a result, the lifestyle choices of the unemployed are severely restricted. Physical aspects that will be affected include housing and diet.

Emotionally, unemployed individuals may feel a sense of worthlessness and their self-concept can be lowered. Individuals might blame themselves for their situation and suffer from depression. The unemployed can be restricted socially due to the lower level of income. Being unable to join friends in social activities, for example, going clubbing or to a football match, might exclude unemployed individuals from their peers.

Intellectually, unemployed people may become bored with the lack of mental stimulation that work provides. Some people, however, may use their free time for further study to gain new or better skills and qualifications. This can improve their future employment prospects.

A person's age may be a significant factor in the response to unemployment. A young adult may have a more positive outlook on finding employment than a middle-aged adult or a person nearer to retirement. For the older person, with possibly greater family and financial responsibilities, the stress levels may be far greater.

Environmental pollution

Environmental pollution can cause serious risks to health and well-being. Leaving litter and rubbish to accumulate encourages flies, mice and rats to breed.

Flies, mice and rats are called vermin. These vermin carry and spread disease, which can lead to food poisoning or gastroenteritis.

Where **air pollution** occurs due to high levels of tobacco smoke or house dust, individuals may suffer from respiratory disorders such as bronchitis. This is where the airways in the lungs become inflamed due to infection. Carbon monoxide, nitrogen oxides, sulphur dioxide, hydrocarbons and particulate matter are other air pollutants. These come from power stations and road transport. The long-term lung function of up to 57 children per 1000 in England and Wales is affected by air pollution. Air pollution may affect how well children's lungs grow and develop.

Road traffic is a major contributor to air pollution in the UK

Unit 2
Promoting health and well-being

A constant high level of **noise** is also an environmental pollutant. Living close to a motorway with high volumes of traffic, or in a noisy part of a town or city, can significantly increase stress levels and cause tension headaches and disturbed sleeping patterns. Skin conditions such as eczema and psoriasis may also be made worse by continual stress.

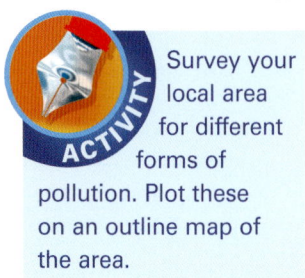

In recent years, we have become more aware of an air pollutant called **radon**. This is a naturally formed radioactive gas given off from rocks such as granite deep in the earth. At low levels it escapes harmlessly into the air, but in some areas it is given off in greater amounts. If the level of the gas builds up in a house, it can increase the risk of lung cancer, especially for smokers who live there. Special pumps have to be fitted to expel the air into the atmosphere and make the house fit to live in.

ACTIVITY: Survey your local area for different forms of pollution. Plot these on an outline map of the area.

Indicators of physical health

There are four indicators of physical health that you should be able to measure. These are:

+ blood pressure
+ peak flow
+ body mass index (BMI)
+ resting pulse and recovery after exercise

Age, gender and lifestyle are all factors that can affect these measurements. These factors need to be considered when interpreting measurements for a particular individual.

Blood pressure

Doctors or trained health carers use a **sphygmomanometer** to measure a person's blood pressure. An untrained person can use an electronic device that fits on the cuff or upper arm.

Taking a blood pressure reading

Both types of device use an inflatable cuff to slowly increase the pressure and stop blood flow momentarily. The doctor listens for the flow to stop using a stethoscope. The pressure is increased a little after the last sound is heard. The cuff is then slowly deflated and the doctor listens to the blood as it starts to flow again through the artery in the arm. The electronic

A sphygmomanometer is used to measure a person's blood pressure.

device automatically measures the pressure needed to stop the blood flow and the pressure when it starts flowing again.

Measurements are made in mmHg — the height of a column of mercury in millimetres. The higher the reading, the higher the pressure. Two readings are taken. The first and higher figure is called the **systolic** pressure. This is the pressure in the arteries when the heart contracts and pushes blood around the body. The second figure is the **diastolic** pressure. This is a lower figure and is the pressure in the arteries when the heart relaxes between beats.

Interpreting blood pressure readings

Blood pressure fluctuates naturally at different times of the day. It also increases when a person is active and decreases when they rest or sleep. Routine blood pressure measurements are usually taken when a person is resting. The figures can then be compared with 'normal' healthy figures. For a healthy, young adult, the blood pressure should not normally exceed 120/80 mmHg at rest. For an older healthy adult, 130/90 mmHg is typical.

Unit 2

Promoting health and well-being

High blood pressure, or hypertension, is when readings are consistently above 140/90 mmHg. A number of readings have to be made to diagnose this accurately.

Hypertension is dangerous as it is linked with strokes and heart attacks, which give no other warning. For this reason, it is sometimes called the 'silent killer'. Low blood pressure is called hypotension. Some individuals have naturally low blood pressure but it can be caused by heart problems where the heart muscle cannot pump effectively, or by dehydration in the body.

Peak flow

Peak flow is a measurement of how fast air can be breathed out. It is usually measured using a peak flow meter, but more complicated lung function machines called spirometers can be used.

Using a peak flow meter

To measure peak flow, the person takes in a full breath of air and then seals his/her lips around the peak flow meter mouthpiece and breathes out as hard as possible in one single breath. The meter records the speed of flow of the exhaled air in litres of air per minute (dm^3/min).

A peak flow meter is used to measure the maximum rate at which air is forced from the lungs; it can be used to detect asthma and other lung disorders

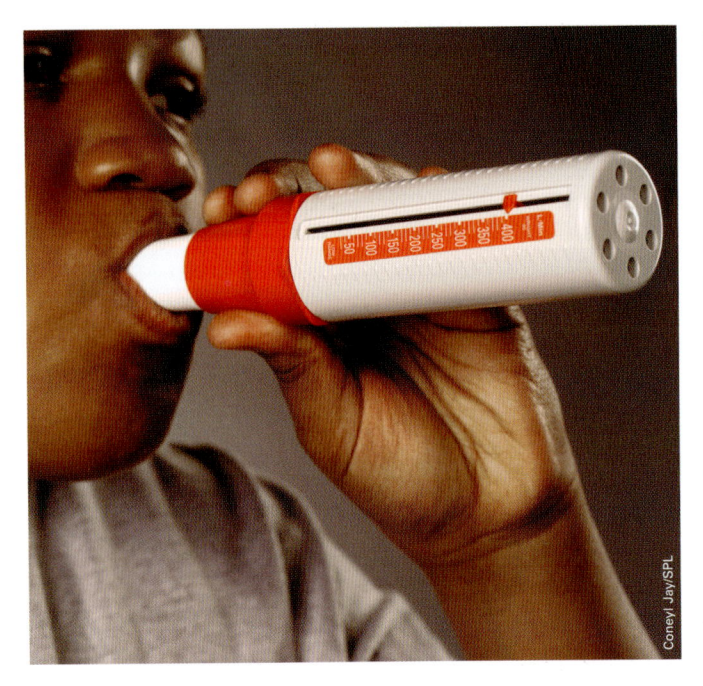

Interpreting peak flow readings

A healthy adult reading is usually in the range 400–600 dm^3/min. Younger individuals and small healthy adults tend to have normal readings below 400 dm^3/min.

People who suffer from **asthma** tend to have readings below 400 dm^3/min. This is because the airways in their lungs constrict (get narrower), making it difficult to move air in or out quickly. When they experience an asthma attack, often linked with cold air, exercise, smoke, or stress and anxiety, the linings of the airways become swollen and inflamed. Smaller airways can be completely blocked by excess mucus. **Mucus** is the sticky substance used to trap dirt and microbes in the air when they enter the lungs. During an attack, asthma sufferers have difficulty breathing and wheeze due to shortness of breath. Drugs can help treat asthma by opening up the airways during an attack or helping to prevent an attack occurring. About 1 in 8 children and 1 in 13 adults in the UK suffer from asthma in some form. This can vary from mild attacks needing little treatment to severe, life-threatening attacks where urgent medical attention is required.

> **ACTIVITY**
> Record peak flow measurements for different individuals. Are there any links between different ages and body sizes in your results?

Body mass index (BMI)

BMI is a useful measurement for dieticians and doctors. It is calculated after measuring a person's weight in kilograms and height in metres. The formula is:

$$BMI = \frac{\text{weight (kilograms)}}{\text{height (metres)} \times \text{height (metres)}}$$

Note: this gives figures in terms of kg per m^2.

This calculation gives a number that can be compared with a BMI table to see if the person is overweight or underweight. There are different versions of the tables. Some tables refer to grades of obesity — that is, grades 1, 2 and 3, where grade 1 is least obese (BMI 25–29) and grade 3 is most obese (BMI over 40). Some tables are gender specific to take account of the slightly different body composition of males and females. No matter which tables are used, a figure below 20 for either gender indicates that the person is underweight. A figure over 25 means the person is overweight.

Female BMI	Indicates	Male BMI	Indicates
Under 18	Underweight	Under 18	Underweight
18–20	Lean	18–20	Lean
21–22	Normal	21–23	Normal
23–28	Overweight	24–32	Overweight
29–36	Moderately obese	32–40	Moderately obese

Table 8 Typical BMI table

One limitation of using BMI as a measurement is that it does not take into account the person's body composition. For example, a high BMI number can indicate a lot of body fat or a very muscular person.

Promoting health and well-being

Resting pulse and recovery after exercise

A person's heart muscles contract to send blood around the body through the arteries. At each heart beat, the walls of the arteries move slightly as the blood passes through them under pressure. This can be felt as a pulse at different points in the body — for example, at the wrist or in the neck. Counting the number of pulses per minute when a person is resting gives the first part of this measurement. It is an indicator of how hard the heart is working. Note: for the sake of accuracy, it is best to take a number of readings at rest and then calculate an average.

How to take a pulse

Use two fingers to feel the pulse; do not use the thumb because it has its own pulse. Count pulse beats for 20 seconds. Multiply the number of pulses by three to get the number of beats/pulses in 1 minute.

Generally, fit people have a low resting pulse. The normal range for adults is 60–80 beats per minute, the average being 72. Very fit individuals may have a resting pulse rate of less than 60 beats per minute. However, a resting pulse rate below 60 beats per minute can also indicate heart problems.

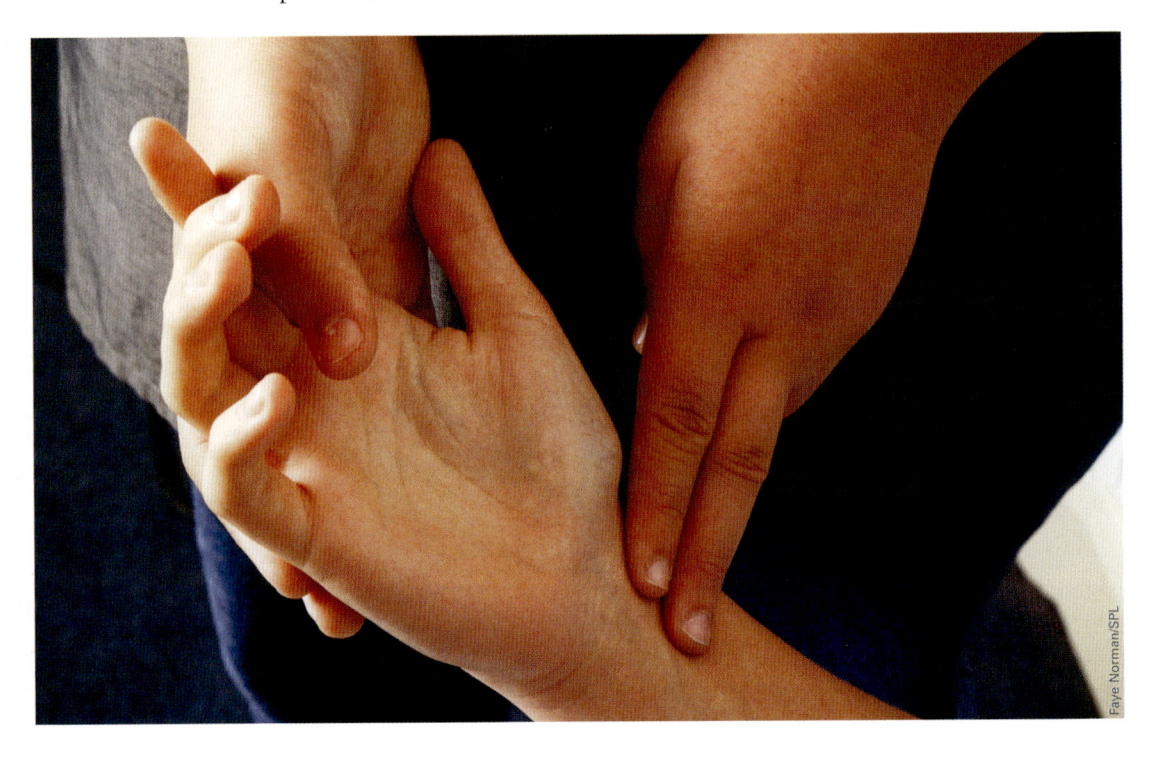

When we exercise or do any form of strenuous activity, our heart works harder. It beats faster to send blood around the body faster and under greater pressure. This increases the pulse rate. The time taken for the pulse to return to the resting rate can be recorded. The faster the recovery after exercise or strenuous activity, the fitter the person.

Note: to be a useful measure, comparative data are needed for recovery rates. There are two ways of doing this:

- A person following an exercise programme can repeat the same exercise at a later date and measure recovery time. If the time is getting shorter, he/she is getting fitter.
- A number of individuals can record their resting pulse rates and then perform an identical exercise before taking further pulse readings. The results can be compared to see who is fittest. Remember that it is not how high the pulse rate gets during the exercise that is important, but how quickly the person recovers.

Remember to take a number of resting rate readings to get an accurate average and do an identical exercise, that is, the same speed of movement for exactly the same time.

ACTIVITY

Measure the resting pulse rates of yourself and a friend. Perform a simple exercise, such as step-ups for 5 minutes. Record both pulse rates every minute after the exercise until they return to the resting rate. Which of you is the fitter?

Unit 2 Promoting health and well-being

Motivating and supporting individuals to improve their health

To help people improve their health it is important to give them the information they need. **Health promotion materials** such as information leaflets and websites can help. These include information about both positive factors and the risks to health and well-being.

Information raises awareness of what needs to be done. It is important that people are able to maintain the good factors while reducing or eliminating the risks to health. For this reason, pulling together all available information, including any measures of physical health, helps give a clear picture. Sometimes what needs to be improved is obvious. For example, a smoker probably knows the serious health risks associated with tobacco smoking and that stopping will help greatly to improve his/her physical health. A smoker who is overweight, eating an unbalanced diet and rarely exercising, however, is at even greater risk of serious health problems. If he/she is addicted to tobacco, it is very difficult to stop. Using nicotine patches, nicotine gum or hypnotherapy techniques can all help.

Setting short-term and long-term targets can be useful in helping the smoker to cut down and eventually stop. Realistic, achievable targets help

Nicotine gum, lozenges and patches can help people to stop smoking

individuals to make progress and stay on track to succeed. Cutting down and giving up smoking can lead to increased appetite and it is likely that this will lead to eating more. This can result in unhealthy weight gain.

Nobody likes being told what to do, so it is important to remember that health improvement advice is just that — advice and not a command. Individuals are more likely to follow health advice when they can make choices about what they do and when they do it.

The assessment requirements

Having learned all that you need for this unit, you can now tackle the assessment.

You need to produce a health plan to improve or maintain the physical health and well-being of an individual. The plan must include:
+ factors affecting health and well-being
+ risks to the individual's health
+ records of the use of two measures of health
+ changes the plan may make to the individual

You may base the plan on yourself if you wish.

Unit 2: Promoting health and well-being

Table 9 lists some important dos and don'ts you need to follow if you want high marks for your portfolio assessment. Stick to these guidelines and you will score well. Good luck.

Table 9 What to do and what not to do

Dos	Don'ts
Maintain the anonymity of the chosen individual, e.g. call the person 'Miss X'	Don't call the person Miss X and then disclose who they are, e.g. 'Miss X (my sister)'
Choose an adult or adolescent	Don't choose a young child
Describe the person's lifestyle — you can 'add' some information to help cover more factors and risks	Don't make judgements in the introductory lifestyle information, e.g. 'Miss X eats an unbalanced diet'; you must analyse lifestyle before making judgements; don't make unrealistic additions to lifestyle, e.g. 'drinks a bottle of spirits every day'
Add relevant information, such as dietary details and activity logs, in good detail, e.g. portion size, variety/type of food	Don't be vague with information, e.g. 'cup of tea' (Sugar? How much? Milk? Whole, semi-skimmed or skimmed?)
Keep data manageable, e.g. a typical weekday and a typical weekend day diet/activity log for a week	Don't collect masses of data that become hard to analyse, e.g. a diet covering 3 weeks
Analyse data in detail for good factors and risks to health (for high marks you should look at two or three of the seven good factors and three or four of the 12 risk factors in the specification)	Don't copy from textbooks or websites and not analyse collected data; don't analyse only the risks to health while forgetting the role of the positive factors
Make sure you analyse the factors and risks for the individual	Don't give general explanations of factors and risks not linked to the chosen individual
Include records of two measures of physical health from the four in the unit specification	Don't introduce other measures of physical health or include only one from the unit specification
Pull together all the information from the analysis when constructing the plan, i.e. good factors, risks and measures of health; for high marks, consider degrees of risk and/or how factors and risks act together to affect health and well-being	Don't deal only with risks in the plan or only cover two or three factors/risks
Include in detail how the plan may produce changes, giving reasons and explanations for these changes and including how the measures of health may also be changed	Don't make vague statements about changes, e.g. 'Miss X will be healthier/fitter' without reasons or explanations of how and why
Provide evidence to back up your judgements, e.g. analysis of suggested diet to show how it is an improvement	Don't suggest changes without supporting evidence

Unit 3

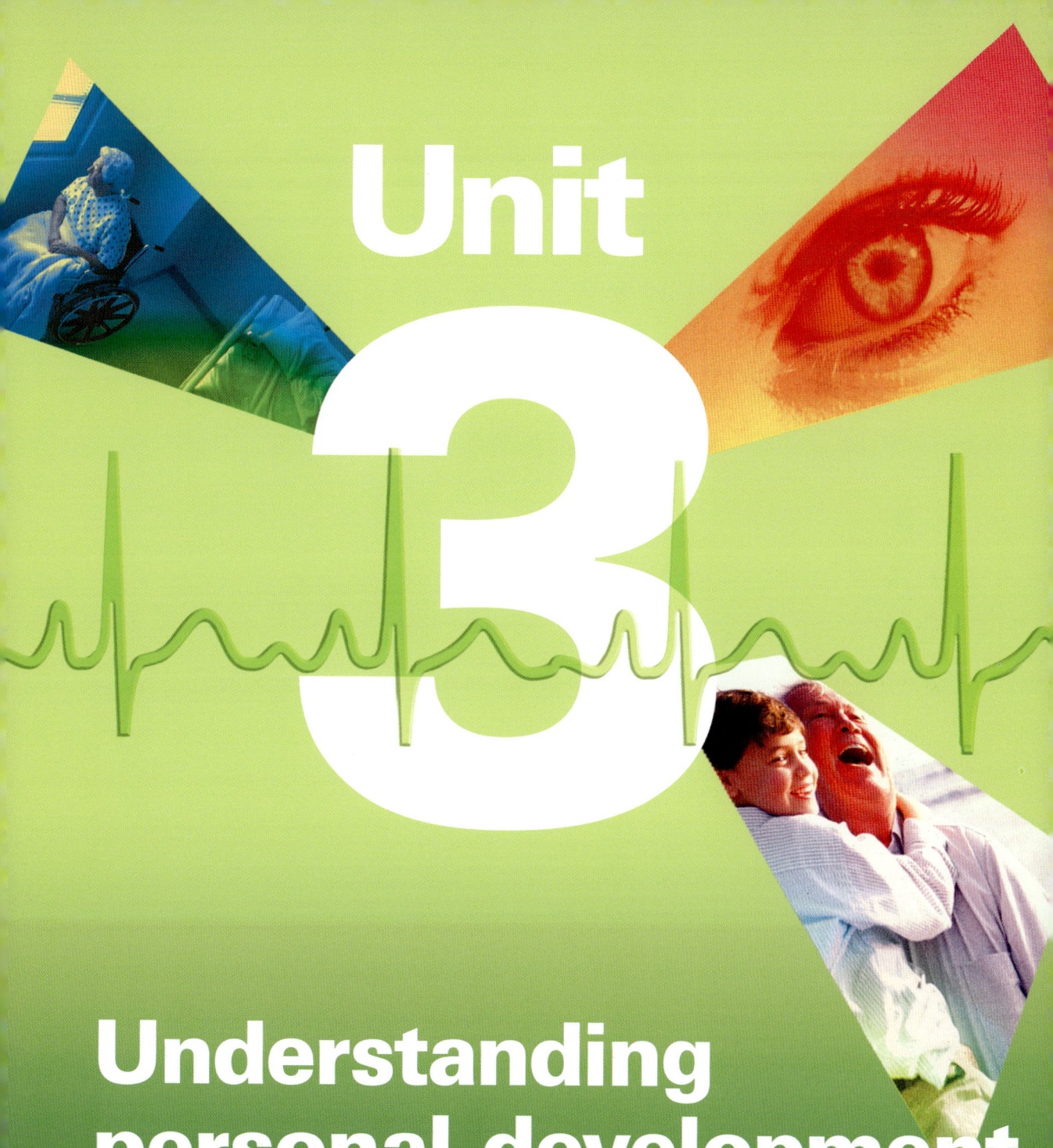

Understanding personal development and relationships

Unit 3
Understanding personal development and relationships

This unit covers:
+ stages and patterns of human growth and development
+ factors that can affect human growth and development
+ the development of self-concept and personal relationships
+ major life changes and how people deal with them
+ the role of relationships in personal development

You need to learn:
+ how individuals grow and develop during each life stage
+ what factors affect human growth and development and how these can influence an individual's health, well-being and life opportunities
+ what effect relationships have on personal development
+ what factors influence the development of a person's self-concept
+ how life events can affect personal development

Human growth and development

When we grow we get bigger. Our body cells divide repeatedly to produce new cells. These are organised into specialised tissues and organs. Our height increases and we gain body mass to increase our weight. At the same time we develop our skills, abilities and emotions. As we are all different, we grow and develop in slightly different ways and at slightly different rates. However, we all follow more or less the same pattern of growth and development through the five main **life stages**.

We can look at these typical growth and development patterns using the **PIES** (**physical**, **intellectual**, **emotional** and **social**) aspects of health and well-being.

Unit 3

Understanding personal development and relationships

Life stages

Infancy

Physical growth and development

Infants grow and develop very quickly physically. Between birth and age 3 years, infants gain strength as muscles grow. The first teeth develop. These are called **milk teeth**. Newborn babies have very little movement, but by 3–4 months most can control their head movements and lift their chests when placed on their stomachs. Body movement develops so that infants can roll over, then sit, crawl, walk, run, jump and climb. These full body movements are called **gross motor skills**.

Infants also develop **fine motor skills**. These are smaller, more precise movements. Handling skills develop, so a pencil or crayon can be held for scribbling or drawing, zips and buttons can be done up and undone, scissors can be used to cut paper and towers can be built using bricks.

Infants in their first year grow approximately 25–30 millimetres each month. By 12 months of age their weight will have tripled. Growth is slower in the second year of life.

Intellectual growth and development

When a baby is born, its brain contains 100 billion nerve cells. During the first 2 years of life the brain changes dramatically by developing connections between these nerve cells. This enables the development of language. From basic cries and cooing noises, the infant learns simple words and starts to talk in sentences. Infants become aware of people and objects and are able to follow simple instructions. They learn their name and age, can answer questions, count up to three and recognise different colours. They remember more and more as their memory develops. Parents can encourage language development by talking to their children often and by reading to them daily.

Learning to ride a tricycle is a skill that most infants learn at the age of 2–3 years; riding a bicycle usually comes a little later

Unit 3   Understanding personal development and relationships

Emotional growth and development

Infants bond with their parents or carers early in life. This bond is a strong emotional attachment. Infants develop trust with their parents or carers. When separated from parents or carers, they become anxious and distressed. When unhappy, they can be comforted by the parents. Infants are able to show affection with kisses and cuddles. Around 2 years of age, they can have temper tantrums when frustrated, but these generally lessen by the age of 3 years. Their **self-concept** develops from the first year of life. As they develop, they become able to express their own feelings.

Social growth and development

Social development in infants begins with the immediate family. Infants interact with parents, brothers and sisters. For example, they begin to smile when talked to or held. From around 1 year of age, infants begin to learn what is acceptable behaviour and what is not. Later in infancy, the social circle widens and infants enjoy the company of others. They develop from playing on their own to playing with others. They to learn to share, and develop basic social skills such as eating with a fork and spoon and going to the toilet. They imitate what others do and say.

Social development in children often begins at nursery school

ACTIVITY: Visit a playgroup or nursery and observe infant play. Look for interactions with other infants and with carers.

Childhood

Physical growth and development

Children grow taller and generally look slimmer than infants. Their motor skills develop with increasing strength, balance and coordination. This means they can do more than infants. Children can skip, ride a bicycle and run further and faster than before. Growth in children is rapid but not generally as fast as in infancy.

Permanent teeth generally begin to replace milk teeth from about 6 years of age. By this time, most children have full **bladder control** both during the day and at night.

Intellectual growth and development

Generally, children can use adult speech at the start of childhood and their vocabulary quickly increases. They can read and write and develop further counting and other number skills throughout this stage. Their concentration and memory span also increase. They will have learnt certain routines — for example, how to tie their shoe laces and how to brush their teeth. They can solve complex puzzles and problems using logical thought, provided they can 'see' what the problem is. This might involve asking questions using pictures of the problem.

Emotional growth and development

During childhood, individuals experience a wide range of emotions and become able to express their feelings well. Self-concept and self-confidence

Older children learn to play together

Unit 3 Understanding personal development and relationships

develop further as they become more independent (less dependent on parents and carers). Other emotional links are made — for example, when forming relationships with friends. Children who feel safe and secure generally have the confidence to form relationships with others. They begin to be more responsible individuals.

Social growth and development

Children form friendship groups during the childhood years. These tend to be with children of the same gender. The groups are large at first but they get smaller. Eventually, one 'best' friend may be established. Children support each other and play together. Generally, their social circle widens when they attend junior school and meet new people. They interact with adults who are not part of their immediate family, such as teachers.

Children learn how to behave in different situations — for example, when at school or visiting relatives. Their behaviour changes as they learn more about what they can and cannot do. Routines such as the school day become established behaviour.

THINK ABOUT IT: How have you changed since childhood?

Adolescence

Physical growth and development

Adolescence is the life stage when puberty occurs. This means that adolescence is a transitional stage as young people move from childhood to adulthood. Girls generally enter puberty earlier than boys. Both boys and girls experience a growth spurt. This increases their height and weight, so much so that body mass can double. Although they start puberty later, boys generally grow bigger than girls.

Sex hormones are produced as adolescents become able to reproduce. The effects caused by the sex hormones are called secondary sexual characteristics.

Table 10 Changes that occur in puberty

Boys	Girls
Sperm produced by testicles	Eggs produced by ovaries
The penis and testicles get bigger	Breasts develop and nipples get bigger
Body hair grows on face, underarms and in pubic area (groin)	Body hair grows on underarms and in pubic area (groin)
Body muscles develop and body gets broader, especially at the shoulders	Body shape becomes curvier as breasts develop and hips widen
The voice 'breaks' (becomes deeper)	Periods start (menstruation)

Intellectual growth and development

During adolescence, individuals attend secondary school and study a wider and more detailed curriculum than in junior school. This develops knowledge, understanding and skills in preparation for adult life.

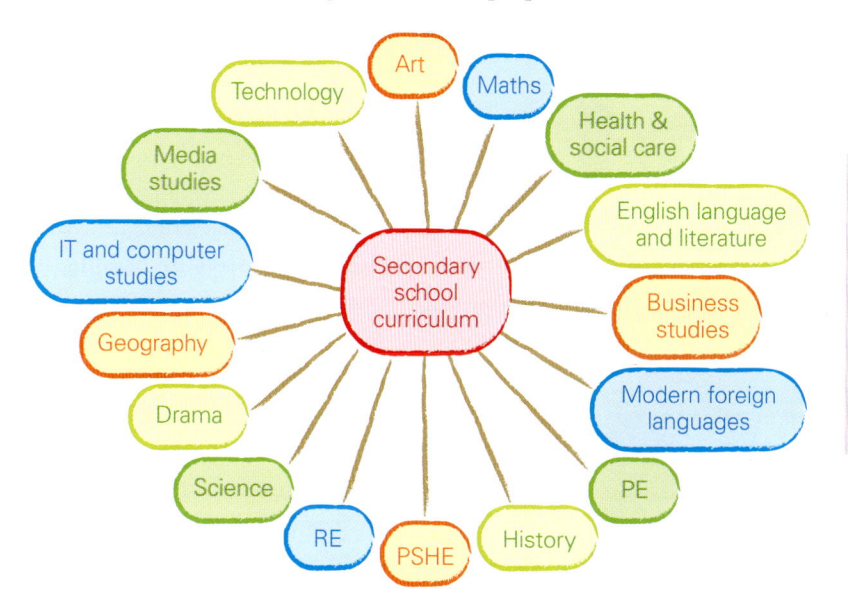

A typical secondary school curriculum

Secondary school curriculum:
- Art
- Maths
- Health & social care
- English language and literature
- Business studies
- Modern foreign languages
- PE
- History
- PSHE
- RE
- Science
- Drama
- Geography
- IT and computer studies
- Media studies
- Technology

THINK ABOUT IT
How is secondary school different from junior school? What have been the major learning differences for you?

During adolescence, individuals' memory improves and they are able to solve more complex problems. This involves thinking logically and often in an abstract way. It means solving a problem by thinking it through, step by step, without having to do it practically. To do this, adolescents have to use their imagination and develop powers of reasoning. It means trying out ideas in their head to find the answer. Often, adolescents will make guesses to start working it out. To think in this way, a person has to be able to think about the future, often about things they have not done or seen before. This is something that children and infants are not able to do.

ACTIVITY
Devise a memory test game for younger children of different ages.

Emotional growth and development

Emotionally, adolescence can be a difficult and stressful time. Hormonal changes in the body create rapid mood swings. One minute the individual might be happy, the next minute, moody and sad. This can have a great effect on adolescent social behaviour and relationships. This is often very obvious in the way adolescents and their parents get along. Adolescents' search for identity may make them appear rebellious. Arguments are common, often about wanting the freedom to act as an adult!

Unit 3 Understanding personal development and relationships

While self-concept continues to develop, it is quite common for adolescents to become self-critical and easily embarrassed. They become highly conscious about the way they look and dress. It is also a time when they become more independent than ever before.

Social growth and development

Adolescence is also the time when individuals first become interested in finding a sexual partner. As physical attraction for a sexual partner develops, adolescents test out new relationships. Close, intimate relationships are formed as individuals 'fall in love' and explore their sexuality.

The influence of parents decreases as the influence of peer groups grows. It is common for adolescents to wear clothes and have hairstyles that make them acceptable to their peer group. This gives a sense of group identity. Hairstyle, or dressing in a particular way, makes a statement about the person. This is often very different from the way parents dress.

Adolescents often adopt hairstyles to fit in with their peers

Each adolescent develops his/her individual personality. Both emotional and social developments prepare adolescents for adult life and the roles and responsibilities that come with it.

Adulthood

For most people, adulthood is the longest life stage. Changes occur as adults age. Young adults aged 20–30 years are at the height of their physical powers. As they grow older and become middle aged (40 years plus) the signs of ageing start to appear.

Physical growth and development

By early adulthood, individuals are fully grown and have reached physical maturity. Their strength and stamina are at a peak. Body systems such as

By early adulthood individuals are physically mature and their strength and stamina are at a peak

the respiratory system and circulation system are at maximum efficiency. The maintenance of physical ability depends very much on the lifestyle adopted. Adults who eat an unbalanced diet, smoke, drink alcohol to excess and do not exercise lose physical capability quickly. They also put themselves at risk of certain diseases, such as heart disease and high blood pressure.

Adults are also at the height of their reproductive powers. Males usually remain fertile throughout adulthood, but females do not. Generally, between the ages of 45 and 55 years, a female's ability to produce eggs stops. This is called the **menopause**. The woman's ovaries gradually become less active and produce smaller amounts of sex hormones. This usually happens over 1–2 years. The first signs of the menopause are irregular periods and heavier menstrual bleeding. Eventually, periods stop altogether.

Other physical symptoms commonly associated with the menopause are:
- 'hot flushes', where the upper body becomes red and the woman feels hot for a few minutes or longer
- heavy sweating, often at night
- dryness of the skin, which can lead to wrinkles forming

Unit 3

Understanding personal development and relationships

In the mid-adult years, around 40 years of age, the ability to repair body tissues begins to decrease. For example, the same broken bone will usually take longer to heal in a 50 year old than it would in a 25 year old.

Some physical signs of ageing appear at this time, such as skin wrinkles and hair loss. These tend to be more obvious and further developed in the later adulthood stage. Eyesight also changes and individuals with previously normal eyesight tend to become long sighted. This often requires reading glasses to be worn.

Physical signs of ageing in middle adulthood include changes in eyesight

Respiratory and circulatory system performance decreases gradually. If an individual exercises regularly, however, these changes can be slowed down. Unfortunately, they cannot be stopped altogether.

All these physical changes during adulthood are perfectly natural and normal.

Intellectual growth and development

Intellectual growth and development continues during adulthood. Individuals carry on learning even though they may no longer be at school, college or university. Everyday life activities provide opportunities to continue learning. Adults develop knowledge and skills at work, just by doing the job and undergoing training. They add to their knowledge and understanding by reading newspapers, surfing the web, watching television, talking to other people and taking part in leisure activities. This is sometimes called gaining **wisdom**. The experiences an adult has can help when facing new problems or when having to make decisions.

Emotional growth and development

By the time people reach adulthood, they will have experienced a wide range of emotions and learned how to cope with them. After the emotional upheavals of adolescence, adulthood is a more stable period. Self-concept continues to develop. Individuals vary naturally — some are confident and others less so. In general, adults are more confident in their middle adulthood years than when they were younger.

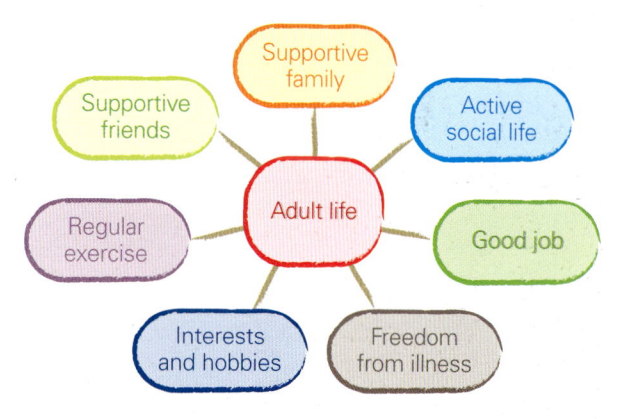

Emotional development, as in any life stage, is closely linked to social development. Having one permanent partner or not, having the support of family and friendship groups or not, and the level of stress at home or at work all have an effect.

The menopause may cause females to become irritable and depressed due to hormonal changes. Various treatments are available to help with this. For example, **hormone replacement therapy** (HRT) can help by replacing the hormones no longer produced naturally by the body.

Emotional feelings in adult life become complex. Adults understand and learn to deal with, or tolerate, different opinions and viewpoints. Where adults have a full and meaningful life, a sense of satisfaction and achievement is developed.

Factors that improve emotional well-being in adult life

Social growth and development

Adulthood is often thought of as a settling down stage. Having learned the necessary social skills, adults generally know how to behave appropriately. Individuals have sexual relationships and continue to develop friendships. Interactions with family and friends, and with work and leisure colleagues build the person's social circle.

107

Unit 3
Understanding personal development and relationships

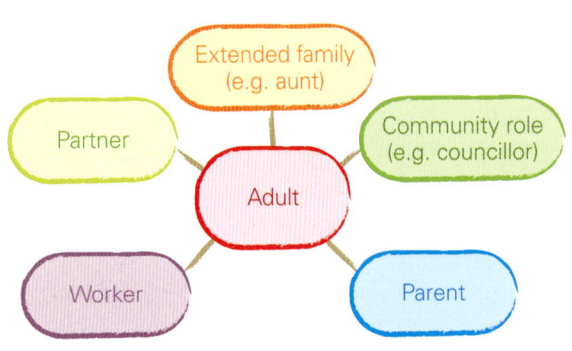

Typical adult roles

While some individuals choose to live alone, most form partnerships of an intimate nature and live together. These relationships may lead to marriage and/or parenthood. Later, individuals may take care of parents or other elderly relatives. Adults therefore take on many different responsibilities and play a number of different roles throughout this life stage.

Each of these roles may compete for time in an adult's life. Balancing the roles can be difficult and stressful.

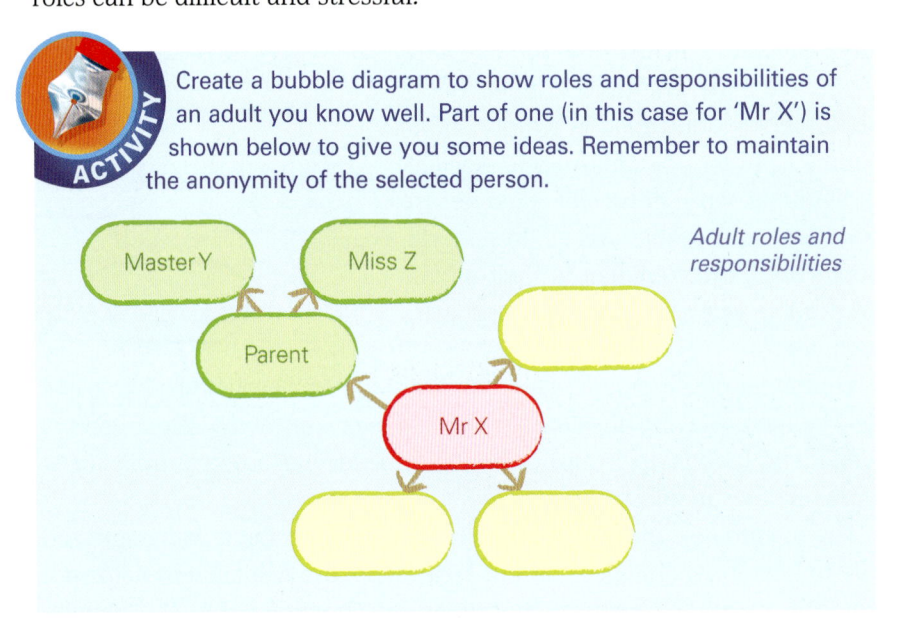

ACTIVITY

Create a bubble diagram to show roles and responsibilities of an adult you know well. Part of one (in this case for 'Mr X') is shown below to give you some ideas. Remember to maintain the anonymity of the selected person.

Adult roles and responsibilities

Later adulthood

Physical growth and development

As we enter later adulthood, some of the physical changes that started during adulthood become more obvious. These include the following:
+ The skin wrinkles as it becomes thinner and less elastic. Brown 'liver' spots may appear on the skin. These have nothing to do with the liver, however. They are sometimes called age spots and are harmless and painless. The skin bruises more easily after knocks.
+ Hair thinning and loss occurs; any remaining hair may turn grey or white.

- Height loss and often some body mass loss occurs; in general, men aged 70 will have lost about 3 cm from their height, while women of the same age will have lost about 5 cm.
- Bones become more brittle and more likely to break if the person falls, particularly in post-menopausal women; the bones lose both mass and density as calcium and other minerals are lost.
- Eyesight deteriorates and individuals become more long sighted.
- Hearing loss, especially of high pitched sounds, occurs.
- The immune system becomes weaker and infections take hold more easily; wounds take longer to heal.
- There is an increased risk of heart and circulatory disease, cancer and stroke.
- Blood pressure at rest increases as the walls of the arteries become less elastic.
- Sense of smell and taste deteriorate and appetite decreases.
- Tooth loss, often caused by gum disease, occurs; the gums tend to shrink.
- Strength, stamina and suppleness decrease as the person becomes less mobile and loses sense of balance; generally, muscle mass is lost as people age.
- Reactions become slower; individuals in later adulthood tend to take longer to respond than younger people.
- The heart and lungs become less efficient at pumping blood and exchanging gases from the air.

Elderly people who continue to exercise regularly can delay the onset of numerous signs of ageing

Most of these changes take place slowly and gradually.

When elderly people continue to exercise regularly, many of these changes can be slowed down. Many elderly people are active even at a great age.

ACTIVITY

Try the skin test with a cooperative elderly person. Gently pinch the back of your hand and then let go. Watch how quickly the skin goes back into shape. Compare how quickly your skin goes back with that of the elderly person.

Unit 3 Understanding personal development and relationships

Intellectual growth and development

Learning continues throughout this final life stage. Many elderly people take up classes and courses, leading to new skills and qualifications, including degrees. Individuals in later adulthood may take longer than younger people to take in information about something that is new and different. However, they do have a lifetime's experiences to help them. This wisdom, built up over time, helps them avoid mistakes that younger, less experienced people may make.

Many elderly individuals suffer **short-term memory** loss. This means they may struggle to remember something that has happened recently, such as what they had for lunch that day. This is sometimes called having a 'senior moment'.

Long-term memory tends not to be affected. Many elderly people have excellent memories of events that happened when they were young. As with physical exercise, those who continue to exercise their minds, for example with regular crosswords and puzzles, slow down the rate of change. Illness or disease sometimes speeds up the intellectual decline. **Dementia** is a disorder that causes increased memory loss and confusion. It affects about one person in ten in later adulthood. One cause of dementia is **Alzheimer's disease** where brain cells break down gradually. Dementia is a progressive decline, that is, it becomes worse over time. It affects memory, attention, language and problem-solving, and sufferers become

Coloured PET scan of the brain of a normal person (left) and a person with Alzheimer's disease (right). Red and yellow show high brain activity; blue and black show low activity (notice how the normal brain on the left has more areas of high levels of activity).

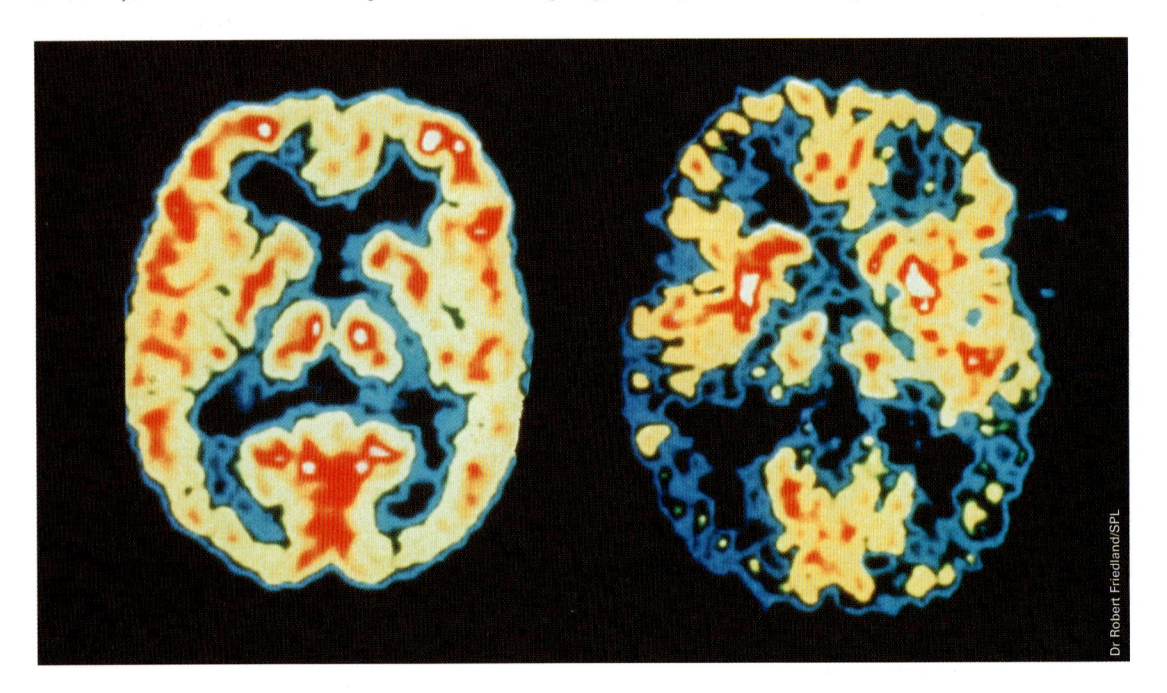

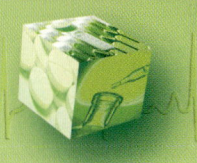

disorientated. Dementia affects not only the sufferers, but also the people around them.

Emotional growth and development

Many elderly people maintain the emotional stability achieved in adulthood throughout their later adulthood. The decline in physical and intellectual abilities, however, can cause some loss of self-confidence and self-esteem. Social changes, such as the loss of a partner, can also make the individual feel vulnerable. It is often difficult for the surviving partner, who may have relied on the deceased for certain everyday tasks such as cooking or driving. The person may become worried and depressed under these circumstances. Professional carers can help in these situations, giving advice and practical support. This enables the individual to maintain his/her independence.

Maintaining an active social life can also help support the person emotionally. This helps to combat loneliness and feelings of isolation as the individual interacts with others.

Older adults often find themselves with a new role as grandparents.

Social growth and development

Later adulthood is a period of great social change. People often retire from work at 65 years of age. This means they miss out on the daily interactions with work colleagues but have more time to spend with family and friends. They have more time for hobbies and interests and may make new friends. Retirement often means a reduced income – living on a **pension** rather than a **wage** or **salary**. All these factors can contribute to the emotional changes mentioned above. The change of role from worker to pensioner may make these individuals feel as though they have lost status. Others may be affected by the family changes that occur. Sons and daughters have usually grown up and left the family home. They may have families of their own, which provides a new role for the elderly as grandparents.

Definition

Pension is money paid regularly to a person as an income after retirement.

Salary is a payment received periodically (e.g. weekly or monthly) as agreed in an employment contract; it is generally a fixed amount for each period.

Wage is a payment received for a specific amount of work; it varies according to the amount of work done.

ACTIVITY

Find out what social opportunities there are for elderly people in your local area.

Unit 3

Understanding personal development and relationships

Factors that affect growth and development

A number of factors affect our growth, health, well-being and life opportunities. These can be grouped together as shown in the diagram.

Factors affecting people's lives

Physical factors

Physical factors that affect our growth and development include:
+ our **genetic inheritance**
+ the **diet** we eat
+ the amount and type of **physical activity** we take part in
+ our experience of **illness** or **disease**

Genetic inheritance

When the sperm cell from the father fuses with the egg from the mother, it brings together the genetic material that plays a major part in the growth and development of the individual.

About 35 000 **genes** are received from the father and 35 000 partner genes from the mother. The genes are made of a chemical called **DNA** (**deoxyribonucleic acid**). The genes are found in strings called **chromosomes**. The sperm provides 23 chromosomes from the father and the egg provides 23 chromosomes from the mother. This makes 46 chromosomes (23 pairs) in our cells. The genes control many features, including the colour of our hair and eyes, our blood group type and whether or not we can roll our tongues!

In general, it makes no major difference to growth and development which genes we receive. That is to say, blood group types A and O do the same job equally well. Sometimes, however, genetic differences can cause disease or disorder. Sickle-cell disease and cystic fibrosis are diseases caused by abnormal genes. These can affect a person's growth and development significantly.

ACTIVITY Find out how sickle-cell disease and cystic fibrosis affect growth and development.

112

Sometimes problems occur not with the genes but with the chromosomes on which they are arranged. For example, an individual can have more than 23 pairs of chromosomes. An extra single chromosome caused by a fault when cells divide to form an egg or sperm causes Down syndrome. Individuals with Down syndrome have learning disabilities and distinctive physical features such as a round face, protruding tongue and eyes that slant up at the outer corners. Life expectancy is shorter, and children with Down syndrome often have heart defects. About 1 in 1000 babies born in the UK has Down syndrome.

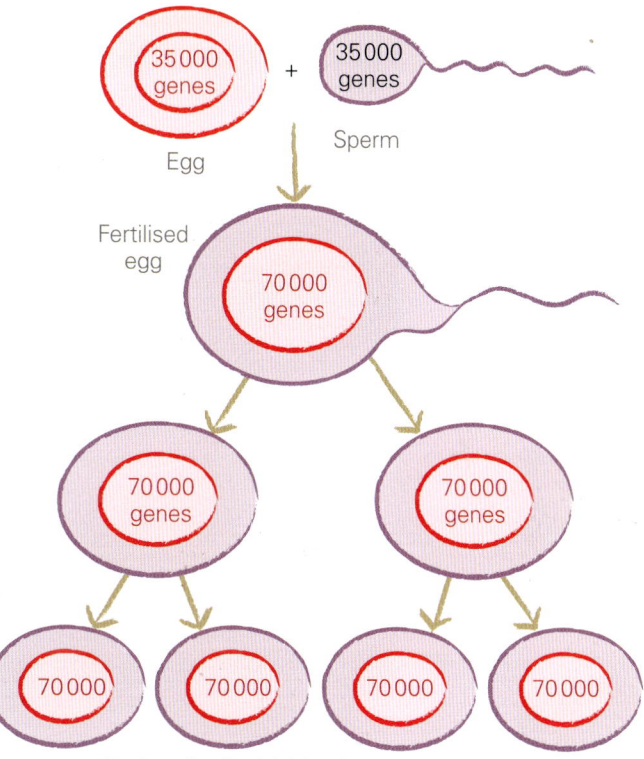

The little boy has Down syndrome

Genetic inheritance

Unit 3

Understanding personal development and relationships

Diet

Eating an unbalanced diet can affect growth and development in various ways. If we eat too much, we put on weight and may become obese. This causes mobility problems and increases the risk of heart disease and a type of **diabetes**. Too much sugar in the diet encourages tooth decay.

High levels of sugar in the diet and poor dental hygiene are the main causes of tooth decay

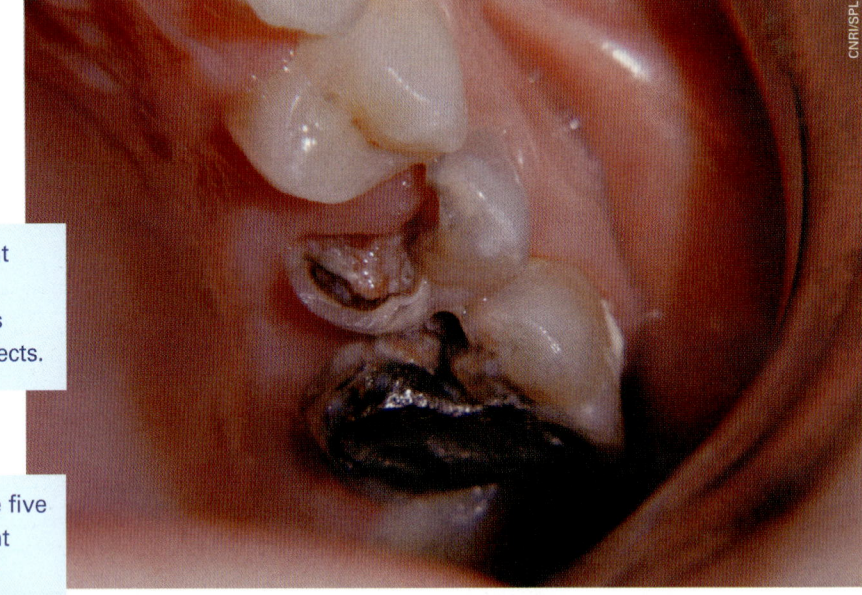

ACTIVITY: Find out about diabetes and its effects.

ACTIVITY: Choose five different fruits or vegetables. Find out what micro-nutrients they contain.

A diet high in salt can cause raised blood pressure, which can lead to heart problems. Too much fat in the diet can also cause heart problems and increases the risk of strokes.

If we eat too little food, we become tired and weak. We lose weight and are more at risk from infections. Not having enough fibre in the diet can cause constipation. Fruit, vegetables and wholemeal foods provide fibre and many of the micronutrients we need. Eating five portions of fruit and vegetables each day therefore makes sense.

A balanced diet is one with the right amounts of:

- protein
- carbohydrates
- fats
- vitamins
- minerals
- fibre
- water

How much food we should eat depends on our age and how active we are. If we are growing rapidly, exercising hard or doing a lot of physical work, we need to eat more.

AQA GCSE **Health & Social Care**

Physical activity

All physical activity needs an energy supply, which we get from the food we eat. So being physically active helps to maintain a healthy weight. Keeping up a good level of physical activity on a regular basis will also help us to stay supple and strong and to have good stamina. Physical activity helps us to cope with everyday physical work and to keep going longer. Shopping, housework, gardening or just climbing stairs are much less effort when we are fit through regular exercise.

Shopping seems much less effort if we stay fit through regular exercise

Individuals who start a regular exercise programme gain benefits very quickly. Even those with heart disease will improve after just 2 months of regular exercise.

ACTIVITY
Start an exercise programme and feel the difference. Remember to start gently and do a little every day, rather than a lot at once. Check your progress by monitoring your weight, or by using resting and recovery pulse rates.

Experience of illness or disease

Everyone at some time or other will catch one or more of the common illnesses or diseases such as a cold or flu. These are generally short-term events and although we feel unwell for a time, we soon recover with no

115

Unit 3

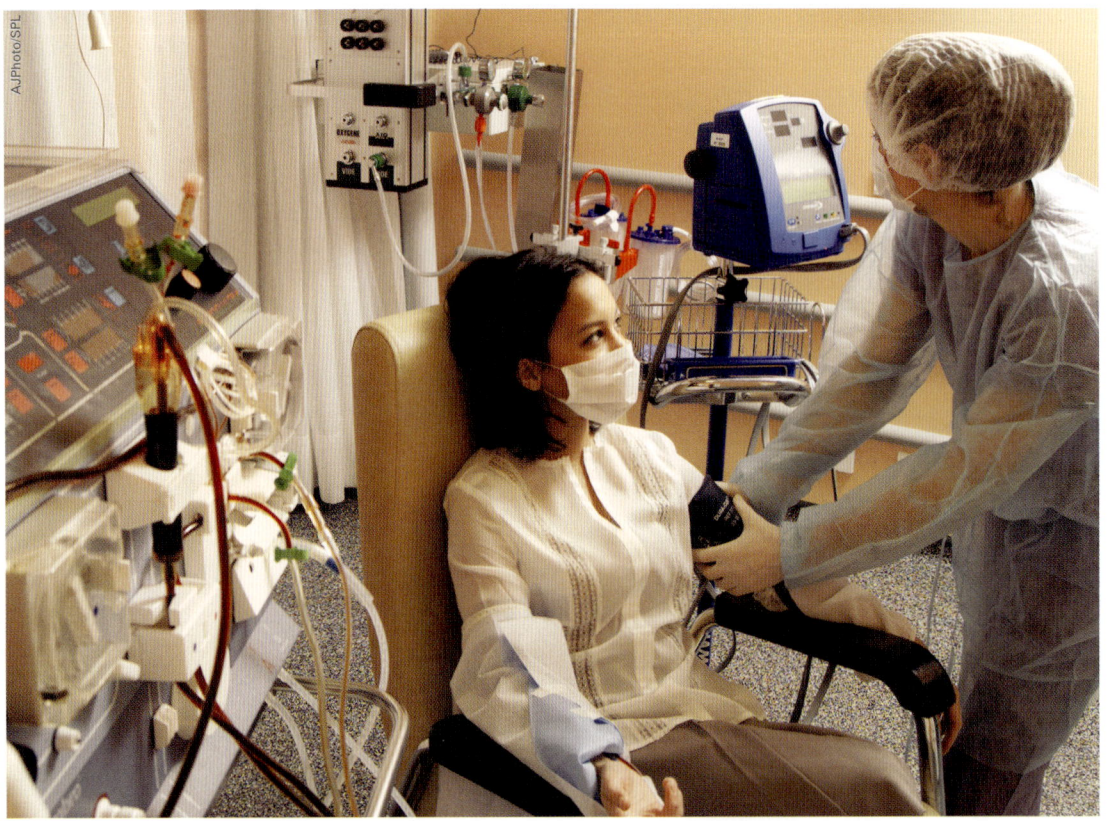

Understanding personal development and relationships

Kidney problems can require 3–4 hours' treatment three or four times every week

lasting damage. Some illnesses are more serious and cause on-going problems. It does not necessarily mean, however, that sufferers cannot enjoy a full and active life. In some cases, the illness of a family member puts extra responsibilities on others in the family who help with their care.

Social and emotional factors

A number of social and emotional factors affect our health and well-being.

Positive experiences in general raise self-confidence and self-esteem while negative ones cause upset, anxiety, loss of confidence and sometimes depression. Positive factors that help health and well-being include:

+ being comfortable with your gender
+ having supportive family and friends
+ doing well at school, college or university
+ having a rewarding career

- enjoying the cultural support of those in the same ethnic or religious group
- having good life experiences, (e.g. enjoying holidays, finding a partner or starting a family)

Negative factors that can damage health and well-being include:
- being uncomfortable with your gender
- lacking support of family and friends and becoming socially isolated
- leaving school with poor qualifications or no qualifications at all
- being out of work or unable to find a worthwhile job
- feeling oppressed as part of an ethnic minority
- having poor life experiences (e.g. being neglected or abused)

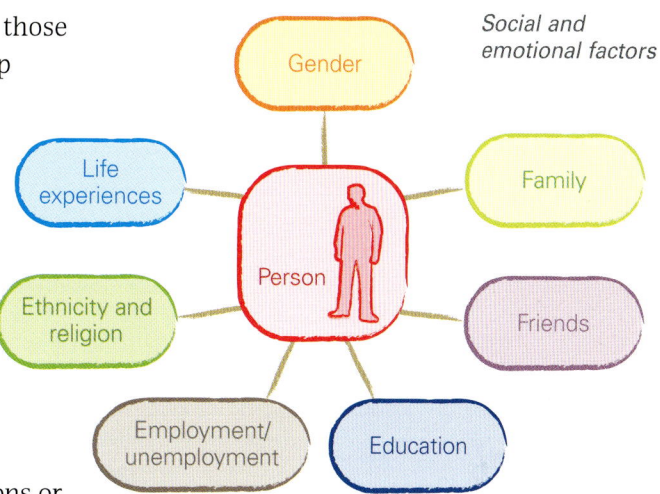

Social and emotional factors

Choose your favourite television soap character. Draw a bubble diagram for the character, identifying the social and emotional factors in his/her life and describing the effects they have.

Economic factors

Economic factors are money issues. A person's income is the money received, usually weekly or monthly, for him/her to manage or spend. People either receive wages or a salary from their job, or receive money from the government (benefits) if they are unable to work. People can also receive money from the government if they earn a low wage. A national minimum wage has been introduced to try to ensure that all workers earn enough money to live. Not having enough money to live is called poverty.

Some of a person's income will be spent meeting their 'needs'. These are the **essentials** that everyone must have.

Needs for health and well-being

117

Unit 3 Understanding personal development and relationships

Wants — non-essential spending

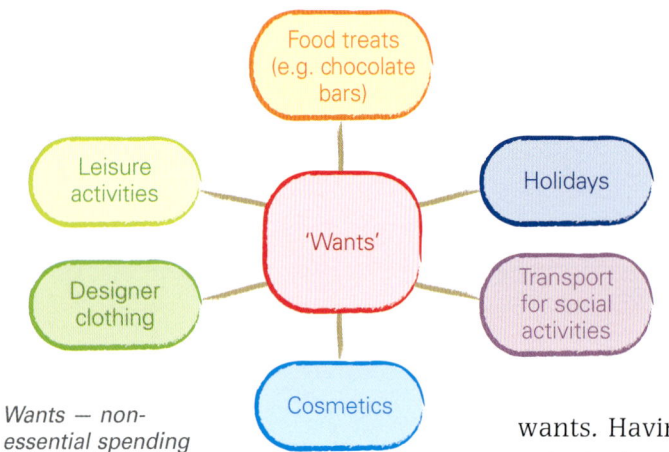

(Diagram: 'Wants' — Food treats (e.g. chocolate bars), Holidays, Transport for social activities, Cosmetics, Designer clothing, Leisure activities)

Money that is not needed for essentials can be spent on **non-essentials**. These are 'wants'. It is important that individuals manage their money to cover needs before spending on wants.

Being able to manage personal spending is called budgeting. People on low incomes may be able to cover all their needs but have little money left over for wants. Having a higher income allows individuals to have many choices for non-essential spending. This is not always a good thing — it may lead to poor lifestyle choices — for example, overeating or 'spoiling' their children with over-generosity.

Living in poverty can cause physical health problems when individuals are cold and hungry, or living in poor housing conditions. It may also cause emotional problems as lack of money increases stress and anxiety, possibly leading to depression and loss of self-esteem. Socially, it may exclude the individual from activities that cost money — for example, not being able to join friends at the cinema.

Having enough money to meet physical needs and a reasonable amount of wants helps reduce stress and encourages contentment. It also means that individuals can enjoy an active social life with friends and family.

Environmental factors

Housing

Where people live can affect their health and well-being. Some individuals have little choice of the type of home they live in because they have a low income. A small minority of people are homeless and live 'on the streets'. Others with more money are able to afford a choice of better accommodation. Key features of housing that affect health and well-being are:

+ the available living space
+ the effectiveness of the heating system
+ the ease or difficulty of cleaning

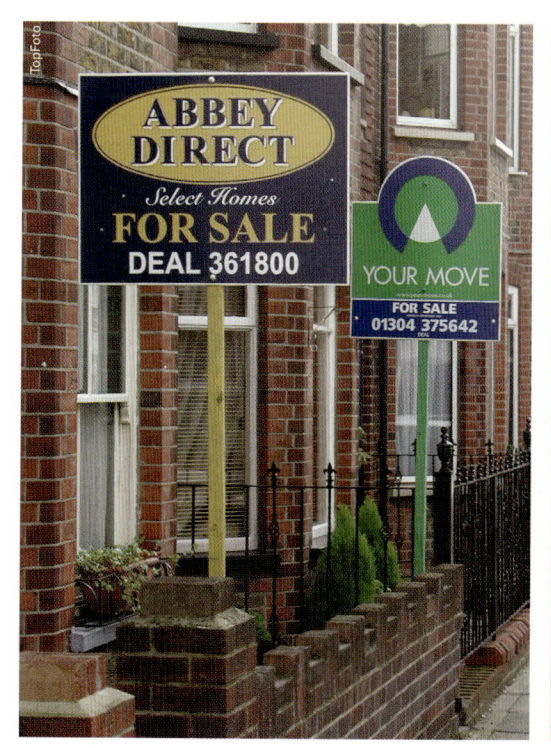

A suitable living environments is important for health and well-being

A small living space, especially for large families, can cause a good deal of stress. This can affect relationships in the family and may damage both emotional and social well-being. Having plenty of room gives individuals their own space for privacy and a chance to relax. Children and adolescents, for example, can benefit from having their own separate rooms where they can do homework without interruption or distractions.

Poor heating systems, or accommodation that loses heat easily, can have a major effect on health and well-being. The elderly are particularly vulnerable if they get too cold. They can suffer from hypothermia. The government recognises that adequate heating is essential. It provides financial help to those in later adulthood to pay heating bills.

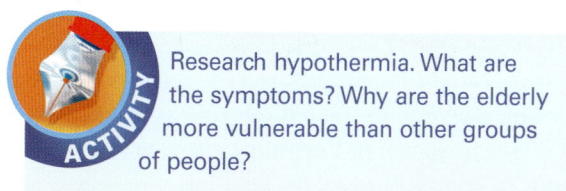

ACTIVITY

Research hypothermia. What are the symptoms? Why are the elderly more vulnerable than other groups of people?

Inadequate heating and damp conditions can lead to mould, which in turn can cause illness

Understanding personal development and relationships

Finding enough money to pay heating bills can be difficult for people on a low income. This can cause worry and depression and raised stress levels. Homes that are difficult to heat well are also often damp. The home can become difficult to clean because of this. Therefore, lack of adequate heating makes living in these homes unpleasant. House mites can be found where dust and dirt collects and these can trigger asthma attacks. Microbes may build up and infections can spread.

Pollution

Common causes of environmental pollution are:

- litter
- smoke
- noise

A build-up of litter attracts rats and mice. These will breed and spread disease if not removed.

Smoke from cigarettes and traffic causes air pollution. Non-smokers living in a home with a smoker are also affected. By inhaling second-hand smoke, these passive smokers are at high risk of developing diseases such as lung cancer and heart problems, which are linked to tobacco smoking. In general, air pollution increases the risk of lung diseases such as bronchitis.

Living close to heavy traffic or in a noisy area can cause health problems. This noise pollution may raise stress levels and disturb sleeping patterns. Individuals may become tired and irritable as their emotional health and well-being suffers under these circumstances.

Access to health and welfare services

Emergency health services, for example ambulance, blood transfusion and accident and emergency departments in hospitals, are available across the UK for all individuals who need them. Non-emergency services, provided locally by the NHS, may have waiting lists. The waiting time for treatment varies according to locality. This is known as the 'postcode lottery'. People with medical insurance or the means to pay have the choice of private healthcare. In these cases, waiting times are short.

Specialist healthcare, such as cancer treatment, may not be available near where the patient lives. This may mean the patient has to travel long distances to access care. General hospital and primary care services are easily accessible in most areas. However, individuals living in remote rural

People who live in remote rural areas may have to travel long distances to access healthcare

areas may find they must travel considerable distances to access even these non-specialist services.

Interrelationship of factors affecting growth and development

Each of the factors described may affect a person's growth and development. These effects may be on the person's:
- self-esteem
- physical and mental health
- employment prospects
- level of education

The factors do not work in isolation. Many factors have a greater or lesser effect depending on what other factors are affecting the individual at the same time.

Example 1 Diet and exercise

If people overeat regularly, they have an unbalanced diet and may put on weight, so damaging their physical health. If they also do not take regular exercise, this will further increase weight gain. Weight gain can lead to mobility problems and greater risk of heart disease. As a result, their self-esteem may decrease, affecting emotional health and well-being. If they regularly overeat but are very active and take a great deal of regular exercise, weight gain may be prevented.

Unit 3 Understanding personal development and relationships

> **ACTIVITY**
>
> Link other factors affecting growth and development. Link factors from the same area, for example physical factors, with each other and also link factors from different areas, for example economic and environmental. Explain how the factors work together to cause effects on health and well-being.

Example 2
Genetic inheritance and relationships

Some people's genetic inheritance may give them the potential to do well in education. If they are influenced by relationships with friends who truant from school, they may also miss lessons. This might lead to poor qualifications and reduced employment prospects. Genetic inheritance is a factor that cannot be changed, but people do have control over their relationships and how much these are allowed to influence behaviour.

Relationships and personal development

Individuals form different relationships throughout the various life stages. When we are very young, these relationships are almost entirely with parents and other members of our immediate family. As we grow up, we meet and form relationships with people in different situations. For example, at school we meet new people, make friends, and form relationships with teachers and other adults.

Later, we interact with work colleagues. Some of these individuals will be peers. This means they are of equal status in the relationship — for example, two care assistants working in a residential home are peers. Other working relationships include employer/employee and teacher/student. In these cases, the individuals are not of equal status. When individuals form close friendships, intimate, personal and sexual relationships may develop.

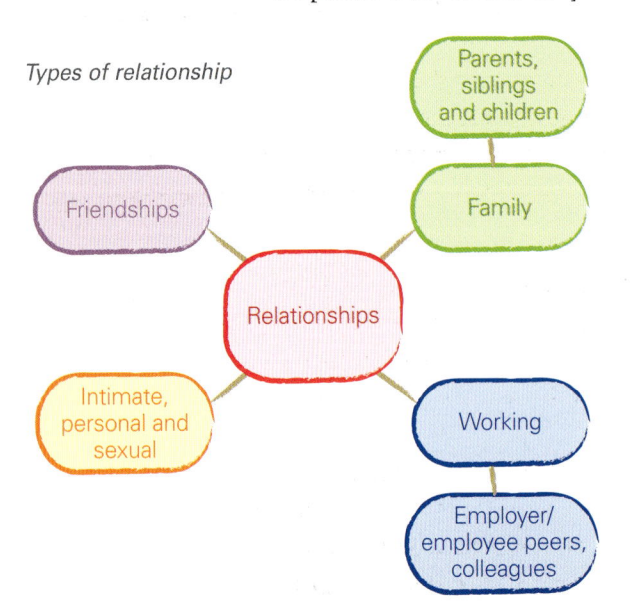

Relationships can have positive or negative effects on personal development. Generally, they affect the social and emotional aspects of our development. People develop their social skills from an early age. We learn how to interact and hold a conversation with others. We support one another by listening and

Types of relationship

- Relationships
  - Friendships
  - Family
    - Parents, siblings and children
  - Intimate, personal and sexual
  - Working
    - Employer/employee peers, colleagues

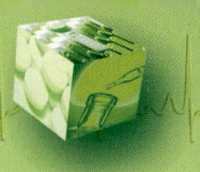

Teachers form relationships with other teachers and with their students

talking. We develop a sense of trust and security as we share our thoughts. When problems occur in relationships, however, the usual negative effects are upset, anxiety and increased stress. In extreme cases, **abuse**, neglect and lack of support can occur. Abuse occurs when one or more individuals in a relationship cause harm to another person. Abuse could be:

+ **physical**, where one person is violent towards another person
+ **sexual**, where an individual is forced into improper sexual activity
+ **emotional** or **psychological**, where an individual inflicts non-violent but emotional pain on another

Children are often vulnerable partners in relationships and may be subject to abuse. When a child is **neglected**, that is, not properly cared for, this is another form of abuse. Lacking the proper support may also seriously damage individuals who are not able to look after themselves, such as very elderly people.

Abuse can affect all aspects of personal development. Physical pain, emotional damage in terms of loss of confidence, reduced self-esteem, becoming socially withdrawn and failing to develop intellectually to full potential are all possible effects of abuse.

Unit 3

Understanding personal development and relationships

Factors that influence self-concept

Self-concept is how we see ourselves. It develops from when we are 1–2 years of age and, as we grow older, it is shaped by all the factors in the diagram.

Factors that influence self-concept

Factors surrounding Self-concept: Life experiences, Age, Appearance, Gender, Culture, Emotional development, Education, Relationships with others, Sexual orientation.

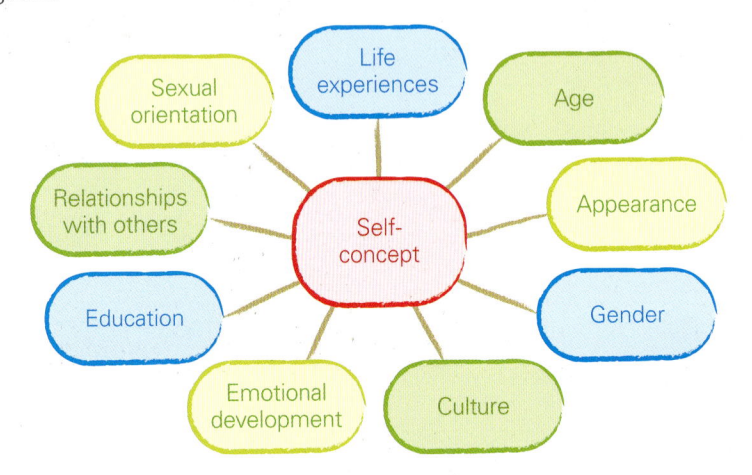

Individuals with a generally positive self-concept tend to be self-confident, motivated, free from anxiety and happy. Individuals with a generally negative self-concept tend to lack confidence and motivation and may feel more anxious and less happy about dealing with life. However, these are generalisations; individuals vary considerably and self-concept is usually a mixture of positive and negative feelings. Self-concept changes over time as different factors exert their influence and the person develops.

At first, young children become aware of themselves as individuals and, a little later, as a boy, or a girl. Generally, confidence increases with age, but some elderly individuals lose confidence, especially if their health fails. In the later stages of childhood and into adolescence, appearance becomes an important factor as individuals become aware of how they are similar to, or different from, others. Being comfortable or not with your gender and sexual orientation also raises or lowers confidence and self-esteem.

Individuals from different cultures develop different beliefs and values. These may influence the way they see themselves. Individuals may feel supported by their culture and develop a positive self-concept by being part of the group.

Educational success in gaining qualifications and improving career opportunities improves self-concept. Individuals with the support of family

A positive self-concept can develop from being part of a group

and friends develop confidence and positive self-concepts. Those who are lonely, socially isolated and lacking the support of others may lose confidence and ask the question, 'what is wrong with me?'

Those who have developed emotionally into mature individuals generally gain the respect of others and this supports a positive self-image. Immature individuals may find themselves treated with a lack of respect, which tends to reduce their self-confidence. Positive or negative life experiences also have significant effects. For example, being promoted at work will boost confidence and self-esteem; redundancy and not being able to find employment will have the opposite effect.

The effects of life events on personal development

Life events can be expected or unexpected. These can have a major impact on an individual's personal development. Expected life events include:

- starting and leaving school
- starting work
- getting married
- having children
- leaving home
- puberty
- menopause
- retirement
- moving house

Unit 3 Understanding personal development and relationships

Unexpected life events include:
- divorce
- serious accident or injury
- redundancy or unemployment
- bereavement
- a big lottery win
- serious illness
- being disabled

Some life events cause significant physical changes – for example, puberty and serious accidents. Other events, such as marriage and divorce, alter relationships. Events such as starting work or redundancy change life circumstances.

Whether events are expected or unexpected, they can cause significant changes to an individual's development. These effects can be physical, intellectual, emotional and/or social. Starting or leaving school, or starting work for the first time, gives new social opportunities. Emotionally, it can be both an exciting and an anxious time. Relationship changes, such as getting married and having children alter social roles for the individuals concerned. Strong emotional bonds are made between the partners and between them and the new baby.

Puberty and the menopause bring about physical and emotional effects due to changing hormone levels in the body. **Retirement** may be looked forward to as the longest holiday in a person's life. However, it can also mean a reduced income as individuals have to live on a pension rather than a salary or wage. This can cause anxiety and fear for the future. Moving house or leaving home presents a challenge and can be stressful. Fortunately, most people settle in quickly and enjoy their new surroundings. This means the emotional upset is short-lived.

Divorce is a relationship change that causes major effects on many different aspects of people's lives. Emotionally, they may feel angry, upset, anxious and resentful. Socially, they may become isolated and withdrawn, possibly losing contact with friends. Friends may take sides to support one or other of the couple. Social opportunities may also change, as divorcees may not be able to socialise in situations where previously they had done so as part of a couple. Physically, the upset may affect eating. This could be a loss of appetite or a tendency to 'binge' eat. Sleeping patterns are also likely to be disturbed. Intellectually, individuals may find it difficult to concentrate or think clearly due to the stress they are experiencing. In addition to all these effects, divorce may mean moving house and adapting to changed financial circumstances. Some couples divorce amicably, recognising that the separation will lower stress levels and the upset caused by numerous disagreements and arguments.

Bereavement, especially the loss of a close friend or relative, causes similar physical, intellectual, emotional and social effects. The shock of a partner's death can cause a total lack of motivation to participate in even basic life activities. The person may become withdrawn and isolated.

Serious **accidents** or **injuries** can cause lasting physical effects, such as problems with mobility. This in turn can limit social activities — for example, not being able to do what friends do. Emotionally, self-confidence and self-esteem may be lowered by reduced physical abilities. Serious illness or disability may cause similar effects. Many disabled people, however, lead full and active lives despite their disabilities.

Redundancy or **unemployment** generally causes emotional effects of loss, anger and worry. The financial payment from redundancy may help in some circumstances, but unless these individuals are ready to retire from work, they will be concerned for the future. Ongoing unemployment can lead to boredom and loss of self-confidence and self-esteem.

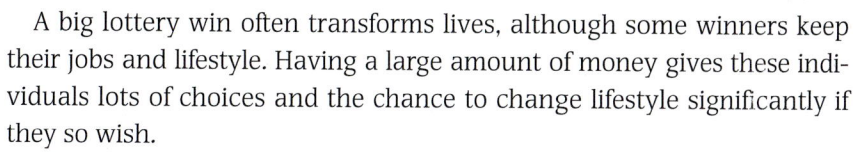

Many disabled people lead full and active lives

A big lottery win often transforms lives, although some winners keep their jobs and lifestyle. Having a large amount of money gives these individuals lots of choices and the chance to change lifestyle significantly if they so wish.

Whatever changes occur in life, people generally adapt and cope successfully with the effects. Sometimes, however, individuals need the support of others to be able to do this.

Sources of support

Sources of support for individuals trying to cope with life events include:
+ partners, family and friends
+ professional carers and services
+ voluntary and faith-based services

Unit 3 Understanding personal development and relationships

Informal care

Partners, family and friends are informal carers. They do not receive pay for the care they supply. Informal carers generally help an individual with daily living tasks.

Help from informal carers

Informal carers help with: Getting up or returning to bed, Personal hygiene, Cleaning, Gardening, Shopping, Transport, Socialising, Cooking, Dressing.

For many individuals, informal care is essential to enable them to live full and active lives. There are nearly 6 million informal carers in the UK. Generally, there are more women carers than men. Most individuals can expect to provide informal care at some point in their lives. By the age of 75, almost two-thirds of all women and nearly half of all men will have provided one or more periods of informal care of at least 20 hours a week.

Professional care

Professional carers are paid workers and are, therefore, formal carers. Some are health workers while others provide social care. Professional carers provide more specialist care services than informal carers are able to give (see Table 11).

Table 11 Professional carers and how they help

Professional carers	What they can do to help
GPs	Diagnose, advise, prescribe medication, refer patients to other services, perform minor surgery
Community/district nurses	Administer medication (e.g. injections), change dressings, advise parents
Health visitors	Advise on healthy lifestyle, advise young mothers on feeding, safety, physical and emotional aspects of childcare and development
Physiotherapists	Provide exercise and treatment to improve mobility
Occupational therapists	Advise on aids and adaptations to the home to help everyday living
Social workers	Assess needs and care management
Counsellors	Listen, reflect, share thoughts and offer advice, teach skills relating to health and well-being issues

Voluntary and faith-based services

Voluntary and faith-based services support many different individuals during times of change. Some of the national voluntary services and what they do are shown in Table 12.

Voluntary services	What they can do to help
Women's Royal Voluntary Service (WRVS)	Meal delivery, home library service, good neighbour scheme, assisted shopping
Age Concern	Advice for the elderly on health and safety, dealing with debt, heating, and accessing care services
Relate	Advice and relationship counselling
Cruse	Counselling and support care, information and advice on bereavement
Citizens' Advice	Information and advice on legal, money and other matters

Table 12
Voluntary services and how they help

Carers help the individual to be as independent as possible

In addition to these large-scale voluntary services, many smaller local services exist to help meet specific needs. Local faith-based groups are also often involved. Typically, these smaller groups provide assistance with daily living tasks, transport and social support for those in need, in much the same way as informal carers do. They are particularly important for individuals who have little or no access to family and friends for informal care.

Individuals can become over-dependent on their carers. This means that, without their carer's help, they may not be able to cope, despite having the ability to do so. It is therefore important that carers help these individuals to be as independent as possible by encouraging them to do as much as they can for themselves. This will also help to maintain the individuals' self-confidence and self-esteem.

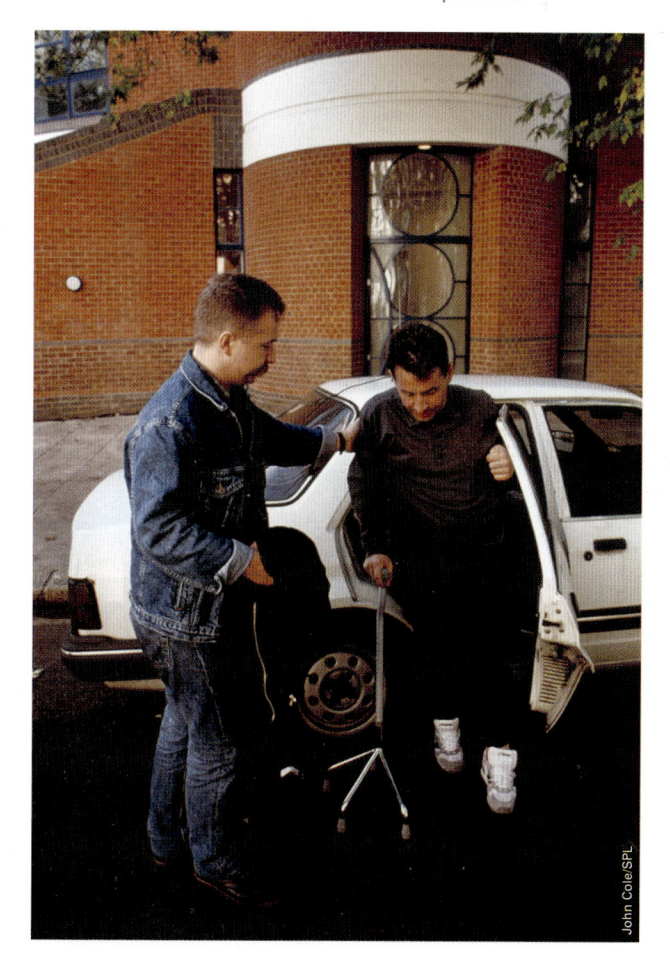

129

Unit 3 Understanding personal development and relationships

The assessment requirements

Now that you have covered what you need to know about this unit, you can prepare for the assessment. This unit is assessed through a written paper of $1\frac{1}{2}$ hours. There are usually 90–96 marks available. Some questions require short answers; others are structured into sections and others need longer, free responses. The questions are organised to test you on your ability to recall and apply knowledge, skills and understanding of the unit content to different scenarios. You are also expected to evaluate evidence, make reasoned judgements and present appropriate conclusions accurately.

These are some important dos and don'ts you need to follow if you want to score high marks and get a good grade in the test. Stick to these dos and don'ts, revise and answer carefully and you will do well.

Table 13
What to do and what not to do

Dos	Don'ts
Take time to read the questions carefully and do the 'easy' ones first	Don't start at question 1 without reading the paper through, or do the 'hard' questions first — you might get upset and lose confidence
Look at the mark allocation for each question — e.g. 3 marks needs three ideas for full marks	Don't answer without looking at the mark allocation — you may not give enough detail in your answer
Check the command verb — identify (select some of the information from the question), name, describe, explain, analyse and evaluate are asking for increasing detail in that order; make sure your answers give the detail required	Don't rewrite the question as an answer; the only time to copy some of the question information in this way is when answering 'identify' questions; for all other types of question, you must add information from what you know and understand
For longer answers, make a simple plan; it is a good way to check that you get all your ideas in and helps the marker know what you intend	Don't just write out a longer answer without planning it — you may repeat points or miss things out and lose marks you could have scored
Try to get 'technical' spellings correct — quality of written communication matters	Don't be careless with spellings, as this may cost you marks
Keep your answers clear and legible; if you make a mistake, cross out with a single line and rewrite; if you have no room, find space at the end of the paper but do mark the question number by your answer	Don't scribble out or try to amend a mistake so that it makes the answer hard to read; if it cannot be read, it cannot score marks
Answer all questions; if you are not sure, make a sensible guess rather than leave a blank	Don't leave blank parts of questions — these cannot score marks, but a good guess might

Index

A

abuse
　emotional 123
　physical 123
　protection from 40
　psychological 123
　sexual 123
abuse of children 123
accident and emergency
　departments 22
accidents, serious 126, 127
acute trusts 9–10
adolescence 3, 102–4
adoption 13
adulthood 3, 104–08
　later 108–11
adult responsibilities 108
advice line 9
advocates 31
Age Concern 14, 129
ageing 106
　premature, in smokers 70
AIDS 81
air pollution 85, 120
albinism 67
alcohol 68–9
Alcoholics Anonymous 14, 70
alcopops 69
Alzheimer's disease 110
anaesthetics 23
anorexia nervosa 74
anti-drugs campaigns 72
assertive outreach 12
assessment requirements 46–7, 93, 130

asthma clinics 21
audiologist 27

B

babies 3, 20, 21
　at birth 99
back pain 79
balanced diet 52
barriers
　to access 16
　cultural and language 17–18
　financial 17
　geographical 17
　physical 16
　psychological 16
　to resources 18
beliefs, cultural 124
bereavement 21, 126, 127
binge drinking 69
binge eating 74
bladder control 101
blindness 18
blood analysis 25
blood cholesterol 59
　tests 64
blood group types 112
blood pressure 86–7
　readings 22, 87–8
blood transfusions 40
body language 6, 41
body mass index (BMI) 86, 89
body odour 78
Braille 18
brain cells 99
　damage 69

131

Index

bronchitis 85
budgeting 118
bulimia 74
bunions 29
BUPA 14

C

Caldicott principles 44
calluses 29
cancer 70, 120
cannabis 71
carbohydrates 52, 53
carbon monoxide poisoning 84
cardiology 23
care homes 14
care, informal 128
care services 3
  non-statutory 7
  statutory 7
care worker
  direct 18
  indirect 18, 37
career 116, 117
cervical cancer 81
cervical smear tests 21, 64
childhood 100–02
childminder 35
child poverty 7
children 3
  abuse of 40
children's nurses 22
chiropodist 29–30
chlamydia 81
chromosomes 112, 113
circulatory problems and heart disease 70
circulatory system 106
Citizens' Advice 129
classroom assistant 36
cleft palate 28
client confidentiality 44
Climbié, Victoria 10–11
clinical psychologist 30

clinics 10
cocaine 71
Code of Professional Conduct (NMC) 44, 45
codes of practice 44
colour blindness 67
commissioning role of primary care trusts 9
communication, effective 41–3
community nurse 19–20, 128
components in food 52
condoms 80
confidentiality of information 38–9, 43
contraception 21, 80
corns 29
coronary heart disease 70, 79
counselling and counsellors 10, 30, 33, 128
CRUSE Bereavement Care 14, 129
cultural beliefs 17–18
cystic fibrosis 112

D

dampness in houses 119, 120
day surgery 10
deafness 18, 27
death from drugs 72, 73
deep vein thrombosis 70
dementia 28, 110–11
dental bridgework 27
dental check-ups 78
dental crowns 27
dentist 26–7
Department of Health 8, 9, 10
development, factors affecting 112–22
diabetes 114
diastolic pressure, blood 87
diet 4, 75–6, 114
  and exercise 121
  overall 57, 58
  poor 74

dietary reference values (DRVs) 57
dieticians 28–9
dignity 39
direct care workers 18
disabled, being 126, 127
discrimination 43
disease 112, 115–16
   genetically inherited 67
district nurse 19–20, 128
divorce 76, 126
DNA (deoxyribonucleic acid) 112
domiciliary care 13
Down syndrome 113
drinking alcohol 80
drug abuse 7, 33, 68
drugs, legal and illegal 68, 71–3

E

ear, nose and throat (ENT) 27
ear syringing 21
economic factors 117–18
ecstasy 71
education 5, 13, 61, 121
educational success 124
effective communication 43
elderly people 82, 108, 109
   abuse to 40
   independence of 16–17
electrotherapy 24
emergency health services 120
emergency operations 13
emotional feelings 107
emotional growth and development
   adolescence 102–4
   adulthood 104–08
   childhood 100–01
   infancy 98–100
   later adulthood 108–11
emotional needs 5
emotional stability 108–11
empathy 6
employment prospects 121
energy 53

essentials
   for living 117
   money for 61
Every Child Matters — Change for Children 11
exercise
   lack of 79–80
   later adulthood 110
   pulse recovery after 90–91
   regular 58–60
eyes
   colour 112
   diseases 23
   examinations 27

F

fairness in treatment 38
faith-based services 129
family support 13, 116, 117
fats 52, 54
fear of hospitals 17
feelings 5
feet and lower legs 29–30
fertility and smoking 71
fetus damage in pregnancy 69
fibre 57
financial barriers 17
financial resources 61
fine motor skills 98–9
food 4, 52–8
food tables for diets 58
fostering 13
friendships 102
fruit and vegetables 57

G

gender 116, 117
   and sexual orientation 124
General Medical Council 45–6
general practitioner (GP) 9, 19, 128
General Social Care Council *Code of Practice* 44, 46

Index

genetic inheritance 112, 122
geographical barriers 17
giving birth 125, 126
gonorrhoea 81
Good Medical Practice 45–6
gross motor skills 98
growth, factors affecting 112
gynaecology 19

H

haemophilia 67
hair colour 108, 112
hair loss 106
hairstyles of adolescents 104
hair thinning 108
halitosis 78
hallucinogenic drug, LSD 72
hand washing 78
health 39
  goals 7
  in later adulthood 109
  monitoring 62–5
  plan 93
  promotion materials 92–3
  visitors 20–21, 128
  and well-being 51–2, 117
Health and Safety at Work Act 66
health and welfare services 120–21
health and well-being, promoting 51–94
hearing loss 27, 28
heart attacks 59
heart disease 23
  and smoking 70
heart muscle 79
heating houses 119, 120
height loss 109
heroin 71–2
high blood pressure 70, 79
HIV 21, 72, 81
hobbies 62
holistic view 52
home care assistant 32–3
homelessness 7

hormone replacement therapy (HRT) 107
hospital doctor 23
housing 118–20
  inadequate 83–4
human growth and development 97
Huntington's disease 67
hydrotherapy 24
hypertension 88
hypotension 88
hypothermia 4, 84, 119

I

identity 43
illness or disease 112, 115–16
illness prevention 62–5
illness, serious 126, 127
immunisation 20, 63
impetigo 78–9
impotence in men, and smoking 71
independence 39, 43, 129
indirect care workers 18, 37
individualised care 40–41
individuals 38–42
infancy 98–100
infant bonding 100
infectious diseases 63
infertility, female 81
informal care 14–15, 128
injections 21
injuries, serious 126, 127
intellectual growth and development
  adolescents 103
  adulthood 106–7
  childhood 101
  infancy 99
  later adulthood 110–11
intellectual needs 5

J

Jehovah's Witnesses 40
job roles in health and social care 18–48

K

kidney problems 116

L

language barriers 17–18
language development 99
learning 5
   disabilities 30, 113
   in later adulthood 110
learning support assistant 36
leisure 61, 62
life events 125–30
lifestyle and health 105
lifestyle factors as risk 67
litter 85, 120
liver disease 69
long-term memory 110
loss of partner 111
lottery win 126, 127
LSD (lysergic acid diethylamide) 71, 72
lung cancer 70, 120

M

Macmillan Cancer Relief 14
macronutrients 52
magic mushrooms 71, 73
mammograms 65
manual therapy 24
marriage 108, 125, 126
marriage guidance 33
meal delivery 129
medical insurance 14
memory improvement 103
memory loss 110
MenCap 14
menopause 105, 107, 125, 126
   and smoking 71
mental health 23, 121
   nurse 21
   problems 5

mental illness 30
micronutrients 56, 114
midwives 20, 44
milk teeth 98
MIND 14
minds 5
   exercise 62
minerals 56
money 61, 117
moods of adolescence 103
mothers and babies 20, 21
motivation for health improvement 92–3
motor skills 100
moving house 125, 126
mucus 89
multi-agency working 13

N

National Blood Authority 9
National Health Service (NHS) 8, 120
   trusts 9–10
negative definition 51
neglected children 123
NHS Direct, advice line 9
nicotine 70
noise 120
   and stress 86
non-essentials 118
   money for 61
nurse 19–22, 44
nursery assistant 34–5
nursery nurse 33–4
nursery school 100
nursing assistant 30–31
Nursing Midwifery Council (NMC) 44, 45
nutrition 75

O

obesity 74, 75, 79
obstetrics 19

Index

occupational therapist 23–4
older people 3
operations 23
ophthalmology 23
optician 27
optometrist 27
oral healthcare 27
oral hygiene 78
orthopaedics 19
out-patient consultations 10

P

paediatric nurses 22, 23
pain control 23
parasite infestation 78
parenthood 108
partners 117
passive smoking 70
pathology 23
PCT *see* Primary Care Trust (PCT)
peak flow 86, 88–9
peer groups 104
pelvic infections 81
pensions 111, 126
personal beliefs 39–40
personal development 97–130
personal hygiene, lack of 77–9
personal relationships 97–130
pharmacist 26
phenylketonuria 67
phlebotomist 25
physical activity 112, 115
physical growth and development
   adolescence 102
   adulthood 104–6
   childhood 100–01
   infancy 98–9
   later adulthood 108
physical health 121
   indicators 86–91
physical, intellectual, emotional
   and social (PIES) 52
physical needs 4
physiotherapists 24, 128

PIES analysis 6, 48, 52
play activities for children 34
playgroup leader 35
policies 44
pollution 120
   environmental 85–6
portfolio assessment 48
positive definition 52
positive experiences 116
postcode lottery 13, 120
post-natal depression 21
poverty 7, 82–3
practice nurse 21
pregnancy
   and alcohol 69
   and smoking 71
pregnancy tests 21
prescription medicines 26
primary care trusts (PCTs) 8, 9, 10
private care services 13–14
professional care 128
professional referral 15
proteins 52, 54–5
psychiatry 19
psychological therapy 10
puberty 102, 125, 126
pulse taking 90–91

Q

qualifications for work 61

R

radiographer 24–5
radon, air pollutant 86
rapport 6
reading 62
recovery after exercise 86
redundancy 76, 126, 127
regular exercise 58–60
Relate 14, 129
relationships 43, 122–3
   supportive 60–61
relaxation exercises 77

religious groups 117
reproduction 105
residential social workers 32
respiratory system 106
respite care 13
resting pulse 86, 90–91
retirement 125, 126
Riding for the Disabled 14
risk management 65–7
risks to health 67
rubbish 85
rural areas and healthcare 121

S

safety 39
salary 111
salt in diet 114
Samaritans 14
schizophrenia 73
school
  and children 102
  leaving 125, 126
  success in 116, 117
screening tests for illness 64
secondary schooling 103
self-concept 5, 100, 101–2
  in adolescents 104
  in adulthood 107
  factors influencing 124–5
self-confidence 101–2, 124, 125, 129
self-esteem 121, 129
self-referral 15
sex hormones 102
sex, unprotected 80–81
sexual abuse 33
sexual partners 104
sexually transmitted infections
  (STIs) 80–81
shelter 4
Shelter 7
short-term memory 110
sickle-cell disease 112
sign language 18
skin ageing 71

smoke 120
smoking 80
  passive 120
  risks to health 70–71
  stopping 92–3
social and emotional factors
  116–17
social care 7, 8
social change in later adulthood 111
social growth and development 107
  adolescence 104
  adulthood 107–8
  childhood 102
  infancy 100
  later adulthood 111
social isolation 81–2
social needs 5–6
social policy goals 7
social services 10–13
  organisation for adults 12
  organisation for children 11
social skills 6
  for children 36
social worker 31–2, 45, 128
solvents 73
special health authorities 9
speech development 101
speech and language therapist
  (SLT) 28
sphygmomanometer, for blood
  pressure 86
spinal discs 79
stammering 28
starches 53
strategic health authorities
  (SHAs) 8, 9, 10
stress 76–7
  from unemployment 84, 85
strokes 24, 28, 70
substance misuse 67–8
sugar in diet 53, 114
support, sources of 127–8
surgery 22
syphilis 81
systolic pressure, blood 87

Index

T

teacher, early years 35
teacher-student relationships 123
teacher-teacher relationships 123
teeth
    cleaning 78
    decay 114
television soaps 61
therapy 30
third-party referral 15
tobacco smoking 68, 70, 120
traffic noise and stress 120
transport help 129
triage officers 22
trichonomoniasis 81
trust 43

U

ultrasound 24
underage drinking 70
unemployment 84–5, 117, 126, 127

V

value bases of care 37–43

vermin 85
verrucae 29
vitamins 56
voluntary care services 14, 129

W

wage 111
waiting lists for treatment 120
warmth 4
warts 29
washing 77–8
water drinking 56, 78
weight gain 79
wisdom 107
Women's Royal Voluntary Service
    (WRVS) 14, 129
work 5, 61, 125, 126
wrinkles 105, 106, 108

X

X-rays 24, 25

Y

yoga 77